Lucky in Love

*To my parents, Nick and Joan Gage, for inviting me to
the party; my husband, Emilio Baltodano, for filling
my life with even more love; and our children,
Amalia and Nico, who make every day a celebration.
And to the readers of this book, I wish you all
the luck in the world.*

Published in the United States by Clarkson Potter/Publishers,
an imprint of the Crown Publishing Group,
a division of Penguin Random House LLC, New York.
crownpublishing.com
clarksonpotter.com
CLARKSON POTTER is a trademark and **POTTER** with colophon
is a registered trademark of Penguin Random House LLC.

Library of Congress Cataloging-in-Publication Data
Names: Gage, Eleni N., author.
Title: Lucky in love : traditions, rituals, and symbols to
personalize your wedding / Eleni Gage.
Description: First edition. | New York : Clarkson Potter Publishers, [2018]
Identifiers: LCCN 2018016479 (print) | LCCN 2018018562 (ebook) |
ISBN 9780525573913 | ISBN 9780525573906 (hardcover)
Subjects: LCSH: Weddings—Planning. | Marriage customs and rites.
Classification: LCC HQ745 (ebook) | LCC HQ745 .G327 2018 (print) |
DDC 392.5—dc23
LC record available at https://lccn.loc.gov/2018016479

ISBN 978-0-525-57390-6
Ebook ISBN 978-0-525-57391-3

Printed in China

Illustrations by Emily Isabella
Book and cover design by Mia Johnson

10 9 8 7 6 5 4 3 2 1

First Edition

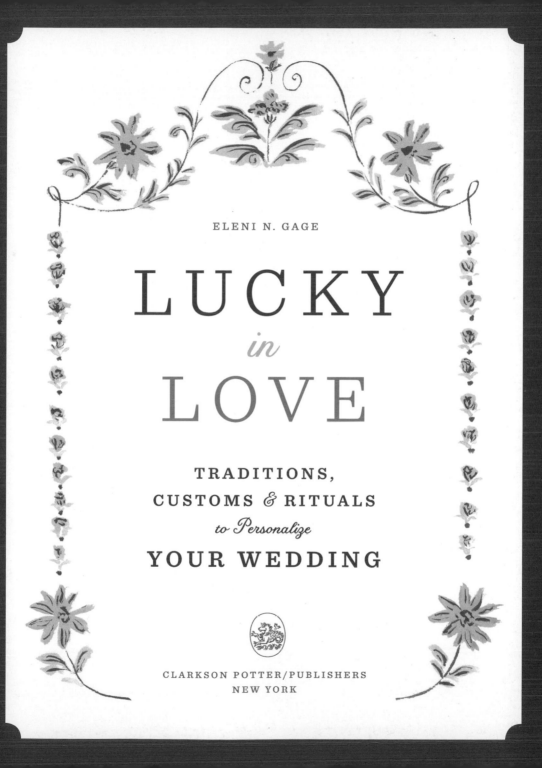

ELENI N. GAGE

LUCKY

in

LOVE

TRADITIONS, CUSTOMS & RITUALS
to Personalize
YOUR WEDDING

CLARKSON POTTER/PUBLISHERS
NEW YORK

Contents

Hello,
LUCKY

WHEN IT COMES TO LUCK, MORE IS MORE.
It's no coincidence that virtually every culture,
religion, and community has devised auspicious
rituals around weddings. In fact, it's folklore—the
traditional practices and wisdom people preserve
through time, then pass on to future generations
to make life more meaningful, and more fun. Most
of these rituals revolve around liminal stages,
life's major transitions, such as birth, coming-of-
age, death, and, everybody's favorite, marriage.

Transitions thrill us, but facing change also makes us nervous. We're all aware that life is full of elements we can't control. This knowledge makes us uncomfortable, so we develop rituals to help us feel we're doing something to tip the odds in our favor, shaping our fate to the extent we can. At a wedding, it's not just the couple getting married who may be anxious, albeit excited, about their future, but their families, too. Regardless of the cultures they come from, most wedding-related rituals focus on the same themes: the end of childhood and the beginning of adulthood; two individuals leaving the families they grew up in and starting a new one; fertility and future generations; and the hope for a long, happy life together.

Major life changes aside, when you're planning a wedding, you could also stress about a million details. For example, will it rain on your outdoor ceremony? Every wedding planning book will tell you to reserve a tent as a backup plan, and that's good, solid, practical advice. But this book recommends burying a bottle of bourbon at the ceremony site before the event, a tradition from the Southern United States said to ensure good weather (and great photo ops). Once you've finished patting down the dirt, you can rest easy, knowing you've done your part, it's out of your hands, and now you can focus on what really matters—marrying the love of your life and enjoying that great party you're throwing.

But calming anxiety isn't the only purpose of a ritual. The repetition of these actions over time makes them feel sacred, linking us to past and future generations. And choosing a few good-luck rituals is also a meaningful way to personalize your wedding. That can be done by incorporating customs from your religion or your spouse-to-be's heritage, or working in details that are significant—and auspicious—to you. If you first met at a Cinco de Mayo celebration, for example, that's a great excuse to serve margaritas and guacamole during cocktail hour.

HOW TO USE THIS BOOK

These pages hold a collection of rituals, customs, traditions—you might even call some superstitions—that have evolved over centuries, all around the world, and each is focused on bringing good fortune to couples getting married. The rituals described here are by no means rules you have to follow. They're traditions meant to inspire ways for you to celebrate your love and extend your joy—and luck—to your guests. Like love, luck multiplies when it's shared.

A good wedding is equal parts planning and magic. Hundreds of other books are devoted to the planning; this one brings the magic. It's organized by phases of the planning process. If you're newly engaged, read through from start to finish; you'll find rituals for everything from setting your date to entering your new home. If you're getting married next week, or even tomorrow, you still might want to start at the beginning, if only to find spiritual support for the choices you've already made. (Your in-laws still haven't stopped complaining that your midweek wedding means their out-of-town friends can't attend? *Don't* tell them that's why you picked it, but *do* inform them of the old English ditty "Marry on Monday for wealth, Tuesday for health, Wednesday the best day of all . . ." and say you picked the date to ensure a happy life together.) Or, if you're at a particular stage in the planning already, scan the Contents page and go straight to the section that applies to your current situation, then read the rest for more inspiration.

There's also an index in the back listing the cultures whose customs are referenced here, so if you're a shiksa marrying a Jewish person, or a *ksenos* getting hitched to a Greek, you can go straight to the pages with traditions that will mean the most to you—or to your in-laws. And, of course, you can flip to your own background to remind yourself of favorite customs, or even discover a few that are new to you. A tradition that reflects your or your partner's familial, religious, or cultural background is inherently meaningful. But you might also take inspiration from another community, reimagining its ritual so that it speaks to you. You may go big with a Hispanic *lazo* ritual (see page 111), incorporating one into your ceremony, or, you could just let the custom inspire you to hold hands as you walk back up the aisle, binding yourselves together that way. Whatever you decide, the ritual should reflect who you are as a couple. You can explain the significance or historical basis of your choices in your program, or keep your reasons to yourselves.

One word of warning. This book is not an all-knowing encyclopedia of global folklore, detailing every wedding tradition ever. Folklore is always growing and changing; there are almost as many rituals as there are families, and they evolve as they are passed on from generation to generation and from person to person. If your community has an amazing, auspicious custom that you didn't find here, I would be thrilled to hear about it; please email me at eleni@luckyinlovebook.com.

And remember, with lucky customs, there's always a work-around. If a traditionally unlucky date is the best one to hold your wedding (because it turns out everyone can only make it on Friday the 13th, say), you can choose an auspicious time of day to wed, and fill the reception hall with feng-shui touches. Rituals and traditions make ceremonies, and life, richer and more beautiful, but in the end, *you* create your own luck. By incorporating a traditional custom into your wedding, you're personalizing your event, but also connecting your sacred ritual to those of countless other couples who have gone before you. What could be luckier than that?

Love is all around.

And luck is, too,

if you know where to look.

CHAPTER ONE

RULES OF ENGAGEMENT

Starting Off on the Right Foot

Chances are, the instant you decided you'd be together forever was a private one. Even if there was a classic down-on-one-knee proposal in public, it's likely to have come after the bolts of lightning and quiet moments when you realized you'd found someone who supports you and delights you and will do so for as long as you both shall live. But once your engagement becomes official and you choose to kick off your future with a wedding, your private promise becomes a public cause for celebration—one with several visible symbols.

ROMANCING THE STONE

A ring has represented the promise of a marriage since ancient times. Roman suitors were the first on record to give their intended brides *annuli pronubi,* betrothal rings, as a tangible marker that the woman now belonged to her fiancé. If you don't like the one-way indication of a woman belonging to a man, consider a ring for the groom as well. South Asian Muslims often exchange betrothal rings, which are worn on the right hand by the man and the left by the woman. In Argentina, couples who are on their way to being engaged exchange silver rings called *alianzas de plata,* then up the ante with *alianzas de oro,* gold rings, when they make the engagement official—a custom that works well with same-sex couples, too. It's only during the wedding ceremony that an Argentinian groom gives the bride a diamond ring called a *cintillo;* he continues to wear his gold band. And in Orthodox Christian countries, such as Greece and Russia, where the wedding ring is traditionally worn on the right hand, some couples place their bands on their left hands when they get engaged, then move them to the right during the wedding. You could reverse the order if you plan on wearing your band on your left hand, or use this custom as precedent for the groom-to-be to start wearing his band when the bride-to-be puts on her engagement ring. And if one or both of you aren't jewelry-wearers, you might adopt the Polynesian tradition of getting a tattoo to symbolize a significant event, or combine the custom of a significant tattoo with the idea of a ring by having a design inked on your fourth finger.

Just as important as who wears engagement rings and when and how they choose to do so is what materials make up the piece of jewelry. Some Indian couples consult an astrologer who will identify a person's lucky gem based on his or her astrological chart and the qualities he or she wants to enhance (creativity, strength, intuition). The same stone can have a different effect on each person, so it has to be a personalized prescription. Astrology aside, in the end, the luckiest stone is the one that makes you happy every time you look at it.

DIAMONDS Now the most common choice of gem for engagement rings, these clear stones have been popular ever since Archduke Maximilian of Austria gave Mary of Burgundy a diamond *M* to mark their betrothal in 1477, but they really took off after a 1947 De Beers ad campaign convinced couples that "a diamond is forever." That tagline is good copywriting, but it's also true. As the most durable natural substance on earth, a diamond is unbreakable, like the bond between the engaged couple.

EMERALDS Green gems, which were sacred to Venus, the goddess of love in ancient Rome, are said to be aphrodisiacs and, not coincidentally, to promote blissful marriages.

NAVARATNA In Thailand and India, jewelry bearing nine gems, known together as *navaratna,* is considered lucky because of the combination of attributes each stone attracts: the diamond brings power, the ruby longevity, the emerald strength, the yellow sapphire love, the blue sapphire wealth, the pearl happiness, the topaz success, the coral good health, and the cat's-eye protection. Each of the stones represents one of the nine major planets in Vedic astrology. In rings, the stones are often set in a circle, or in three rows, with the ruby, which equals the sun, in the center.

RUBIES In Chinese astrology, rubies are linked to luck, fame, and royalty. Plus, they are an indicator of value in the Bible, where wisdom is described as being more precious than the gemstone, and a virtuous woman is said to have "a price far above rubies."

PEARLS Lustrous, cream-colored stones seem like a no-brainer for someone who has a wedding dress in her near future, but the semiprecious beauties aren't often favored for engagements, as they are thought to represent tears, bringing sorrow to the marriage (see pages 73–74). That said, pearls are also believed to cure depression and promote fertility.

SAPPHIRES A sought-after engagement ring stone, these jewels are thought to bring love and happiness to the wearer. Along with diamonds and rubies, they're the most durable gems, which makes them lucky choices for a couple whose love will last a lifetime—and whose jewelry will, too, even if worn daily. If you like colored stones, but blue's not your favorite, remember that sapphires come in other hues, including pink, orange, purple, yellow, green, and black.

OPALS This milky white gem contains colored luster that seems to flash and move, which made it appear magical to ancient cultures. The Greeks thought opals were Zeus's tears (which led to the nickname "the stone of tears"); in ancient India, opals were said to be pieces of a rainbow goddess who turned herself into stone to avoid all the male gods entranced by her beauty; and Arabs believed the gem held trapped lightning. As time went on, the mysterious opal became associated with witches, black magic, and bad luck in Western culture, especially after an 1829 story by Sir Walter Scott about a cursed stone. But opals are considered auspicious in Asia and, in Western countries, for people born in October, who have it as their birthstone. Those who believe in the power of gems also say you can negate the unlucky properties of any stone by pairing it with diamonds.

(SPIRITUALLY) HEAVY METALS

Rings don't need to contain gemstones to announce an engagement. A number of cultures imbue all-metal rings with romantic significance that comes from their design. The Irish *claddagh* ring, which shows two hands holding a crowned heart, can be used as an engagement ring if the crown is facing the wearer's wrist, but should be turned the other way after the wedding. What's lucky about claddagh rings? The design's motto, "May love and friendship reign," and its origin legend: an Irishman was captured by pirates; when he returned home after many years and found that his true love had remained single, waiting for him, he designed the ring as a symbol of his joy. Another lucky option that works as both an engagement and a wedding band is the *gimmel*, which comes from *gemellus*, the Latin word for twin, and became popular during the 1600s. The gimmel has two or three interlocking bands, which can be split and worn by each half of the couple (with the third held by a witness) during the engagement, then joined on the bride's hand as a wedding ring. Speaking of intertwined bands that symbolize long-lasting relationships, Cartier introduced their Trinity Ring, with yellow gold representing fidelity, rose gold love, and white gold friendship, in 1924 in Paris; its popularity has since traveled all over the world.

IT'S OFFICIAL

Once you're engaged, it's time to let people know. Splashing pictures of your ring all over social media is one option. But there are more meaningful, and auspicious, means of getting the news out.

SPREAD THE WORD You may decide to appoint someone to do the announcing on your behalf. In Bavaria, Germany, invites are hand-delivered by the *hochzeitslader*, an official invitation-bearer wearing a top hat who recites a rhyme asking guests to the wedding. If they accept, they take a ribbon from his jacket and pin it to his hat, and ask him to come in for two glasses of schnapps—one for the bride and one for the groom. This way, every invitee gets to have a little pre-party before the wedding.

STAND ON CEREMONY Many religions, including Judaism and Orthodox Christianity, once observed two separate ceremonies for engagement and marriage. If you're having a religious wedding, you may choose to have a rabbi or priest oversee a blessing of the rings at your engagement. For a not-religious-but-spiritual option, consider a Celtic handfasting ceremony, in which an officiant wraps a cord around the couple's clasped hands in an infinity symbol, literally tying the knot as an expression of their desire to come together as one. This practice is common among neo-pagans and Wiccans, who often hold their wedding a year and a day after the handfasting, and choose cords with lucky colors, usually white for purity, blue for loyalty, and red for love (for more on handfasting, see page 111).

THROW A PARTY Today anyone can host an engagement party, even the couple, as a way of sharing their joy. But traditionally, it was the job of the bride's parents. Whoever hosts, there are plenty of ways to weave in good fortune. In Taiwan, brides wear red dresses for their lavish engagement fêtes, as the color is believed to invite wealth and repel bad luck (see page 65). In Rwanda, an engagement party is called a *gusaba*, which means "to ask" in Kinyarwanda. It's sort of a roast in which the bride's relatives make the groom recite tongue twisters, answer questions, and prove his intelligence as hilarity ensues. You could take it as inspiration to have a game night—bride's squad against groom's side—in the lead-up to your wedding.

PAY A VISIT In Ghana, a couple's engagement begins when the groom comes to ask the bride-to-be's family for her hand in marriage by knocking on the door of his future in-laws. If they open it, the wedding's on!

What follows includes drumming, gifts, eating, and a general good time. You don't just marry a person, you marry his or her whole family, right?

In Taiwan, the groom's kin come to the bride's family's home, lighting a firecracker when they're nearby to announce their impending arrival. The bride serves sweet tea with the assistance of a woman who has a good husband and healthy children so that her luck will rub off on the bride. After the groom's relatives drink it, they put a red envelope with money in one of the empty cups. The couple exchange rings (each person taking care not to push the ring to the bottom of the other's finger, as that would be a sign that the pusher will be the controlling one in the marriage), then gifts are exchanged, and a feast is enjoyed.

In Greek families, when friends or relatives stop by to wish you well and check out your ring, it's customary to serve them desserts such as *loukoumades,* honey-dipped balls of dough, signifying a sweet life for the engaged couple. (For this same reason, people of many cultures like to give newlyweds presents that invite sweetness into their marriage— think sugar bowls or honey dishes.)

GIVE GIFTS Aside from rings, certain traditional engagement presents invite good fortune. Prospective grooms on Fiji give the bride or her family *tabua,* sacred sperm whale's teeth, which are rare, very valuable, and thought to have supernatural powers. Welsh grooms-to-be once carved wooden spoons with intricate symbols of love and luck, such as Celtic hearts, horseshoes, and lovebirds, and gave them to their fiancées— a custom that is said to be the origin of the word *spooning.* Today in Wales grooms tend to buy handcrafted "love spoons" for their brides. They may also be given to a couple as a wedding present or anniversary gift, or by them as a favor. Scottish couples traditionally exchange *luckenbooth,* silver brooches with a heart or two entwined hearts wearing a crown. Later, the pair might pin one of their brooches to their baby's blanket to protect the child from the evil eye (see page 89). In the eighteenth and nineteenth centuries, Scottish traders swapped silver for goods with the Iroquois, so luckenbooth became a common Native American accessory, giving the symbol meaning for those cultures as well.

It's not just the couple who exchange gifts. In Holland, the father of the groom will give the bride-to-be a *chatelaine,* a silver chain with useful household items on it, such as scissors, a mirror, a knife, and a pincushion. For many communities, a ritual gift exchange between the two families is the official kickoff of the engagement. In Nigerian Yoruban tradition, the groom's relatives visit the bride's family home to swap money and gifts with her relatives. The groom asks for the elders' blessings, then the veiled bride enters, looks over her dowry, and chooses a package; she is meant to pick a Bible to show her faith. When she opens it, she finds a ring that the groom places on her finger. In Hong Kong, the bride's and groom's kin trade *hui li,* or "return gifts," without the couple there. These presents include tea, lucky plants (such as lotus root, pomegranate, and hibiscus), clothing, and money in amounts that feature the number 8 (see page 32). The spouses-to-be are always present for the Japanese *yuino* ceremony, which can be anything from a casual hang to a formal party, as long as traditional gifts, wrapped in rice paper, are exchanged. These include money; dried foods, such as kelp (*konbu*) to symbolize children, cuttlefish (*surume*) to ensure a long marriage, and bonito (*katsuobushi*) for fertility; a clam shell (*naganoshi*) to signal longevity; a piece of white hemp (*shiraga*) to represent the couple growing old and white-haired together; a fan (*suehiro*) for happiness; and a ritual outfit for the groom (*hakama*). If you're not up to the whole ceremony, consider choosing one of the elements, such as a clamshell or fan, as a décor element to bring in blessings.

CHAPTER TWO

IT'S A DATE

When and Where to Wed

A whole host of cultural considerations can bring good fortune to the when and where of your wedding. If you're still working out these specifics, the traditions and beliefs listed in this chapter may offer some inspiration. But here's a little practical magic to help you choose a day that's auspicious without considering any divination: look to a date that has significance for you two. You might choose to marry on the anniversary of a couple whose relationship you admire, the date you met, or you could get creative, say, picking the 25th because both of your ancestors immigrated to the country in 1925, setting in motion a course of events that led to you finding each other. Part of the trick to being lucky is celebrating luck when you see it.

A RELIGIOUS EXPERIENCE

If you're having a religious ceremony, you probably already know whether your house of worship prohibits weddings during certain times of the year. (Muslims aren't allowed to marry during Ramadan nor Orthodox Christians during Lent, and some Jews avoid marrying between the 17th of Tammuz and the 9th of Av, a period of mourning for the destruction of the Temple, or the Counting of the Omer between Passover and Shavuot.) Otherwise, the choice is yours.

SEASON'S GREETINGS

In terms of seasons, winter weddings have a lucky advantage because a snowy wedding day is seen as a sign of fertility and abundance. Winter also brings holiday wreaths whose circular shape representing endless love, and evergreen boughs, which are symbols of eternity because they're green all year long. Spring flowers can add luck to your bouquet, cake, or invitations—especially lily of the valley, which symbolizes happiness. (For more auspicious floral varieties, see pages 91–95.) Ladybugs, a sweet sign of summer, are considered lucky, both because they eat crop-destroying pests such as aphids, thus helping farmers with the harvest, and because they're associated with the Virgin Mary by Catholics who call the seven spots on a ladybug's back "the seven sorrows of Mary," to honor her suffering during Christ's Passion. If you plan to have children, wheat, pomegranates, and nuts are autumnal symbols associated with fertility because they are examples of a bountiful harvest. (For more food that signifies abundance, see pages 133–138.)

MONTH BY MONTH

Every month has its pluses and minuses when it comes to wedding folklore, and they vary from culture to culture. For example, according to Polish custom, it's auspicious to get married in months that contain the letter *r* in the name, which would be March (*marzec*), June (*czerwiec*), August (*sierpień*), September (*wrzesień*), October (*październik*), and December (*grudzień*). For more inspiration, let's break down the calendar.

JANUARY was *the* time to marry according to the ancient Greeks who called it Gamelion, or "wedding month," as it was devoted to Hera, the goddess of nuptials. (Gamelion ran from what is now December 15 to January 15.) Plus there's a lot to be said for celebrating a new beginning with a new year; a rhyme from the 1920 book *Kentucky Superstitions* states, "Married when the year is new, you will always be loving, kind, and true."

FEBRUARY means Valentine's Day, which adds even more romance to the occasion, as well as Chinese New Year, a lucky time to wed in Asian cultures (though it's occasionally in late January). It's also associated with the month of Adar on the lunar calendar, a fortunate time of year for Jews, as it's when the holiday of Purim is celebrated. Along with the 14th, another popular date to get married is February 29, Leap Day, which comes along only every four years. In Ireland, it was traditionally seen as a day on which women can propose to men, per an agreement between St. Brigid and St. Patrick, according to legend. But it's also beloved by couples who want a unique anniversary and a chance to delay any "seven-year itch" by twenty-one years. Also in Ireland, Shrovetide, the period between Epiphany (January 6th) and Lent, which begins on Ash Wednesday, was considered the most fortunate time to get married, since the Church frowned on weddings during Lent. Shrove Tuesday, the last chance to make it official before Lent, became the luckiest date of all. (Depending on the date of Easter, Shrove Tuesday may be in March.)

MARCH is ideal according to another rhyme from *Kentucky Super-stitions,* which promises that anyone who weds then gets a "splendid catch." And if you envision a life of happy travels together, you'll love the old English rhyme from *Every Woman's Encyclopaedia,* published in 1910–12: "Married when March winds shrill and roar / Your home will lie on a distant shore."

APRIL makes for a memorable date if you lean into the custom of April Fools' Day, celebrating your status as fools for love and incorporating fish symbols in your décor. In France April 1st is called *poisson d'avril,* in Italy, where it's *pesce d'aprile,* kids tape paper fish to the backs of people they have tricked. Late April (or sometimes early May) brings the spring festival celebrated by Hindus and Jains, which is called Akshaya Tritiya, "the third day of unending prosperity"—always a good thing.

MAY is usually the month in which Pentecost, the holiday that commemorates the appearance of the Holy Spirit to the Apostles, occurs. Also known as Whitsunday, the celebration, on the seventh Sunday after Easter, is considered a lucky day to wed in Sweden, where churches are decorated in red to represent the Holy Spirit. But many European cultures once warned against marrying in May, lest you be driven mad by spring fever and make a poor decision. On May 1, ancient Romans celebrated Floralia, a festival for the goddess of flowers, and Celtic pagans observed Beltane, a fertility festival halfway between the spring equinox and the summer solstice. The Celts danced around a maypole topped with a floral "May wreath," versions of which would be lovely in flower girls' hair or on chair backs. You could also bring back the nineteenth- and early-twentieth-century American custom of May baskets—little baskets of flowers children would leave on neighbors' doorsteps on May 1—by giving them as favors.

JUNE has been synonymous with weddings since ancient Rome; the month was named for Juno, the Roman goddess of marriage. The Druids considered the midsummer solstice—the day with the most sunlight each year, falling between June 19 and 25—the wedding of heaven and earth. Today, in countries from Sweden to Brazil, midsummer brings bonfire festivals to drive off evil spirits and celebrate the sun's transit. The occasion is also associated with fertility—consider the Swedish saying, "midsummer's night isn't long but it sets many cradles rocking."

JULY and **AUGUST** are the most popular months for Americans to marry, and each year one or the other contains one of the luckiest days to wed in the Jewish calendar, Tu B'Av. According to Talmudic lore, the 15th day of Av was the beginning of the grape harvest, when single women, dressed in white, would pray and dance in the fields, and men would join them in search of worthy wives. Today, in Israel, it's a Valentine's Day–like celebration of romance. As the eighth month, August is the good-luck jackpot as far as many Asian cultures are concerned (see page 32); August 8th would be doubly lucky. But in Taiwan, the first fifteen days of the seventh lunar month (which roughly includes the second half of August and first half of September) are called Ghost Month, when restless souls return to earth, making celebrations inappropriate.

SEPTEMBER, the ninth month, is fortunate in Chinese culture, as the word for nine (*gáu* in Cantonese) is a homonym for "enduring." And the old English verse in *Every Woman's Encyclopaedia* promises, "Marry in September's shine / Your living will be fair and fine."

OCTOBER means beautiful weather and foliage in much of the world, but has a mixed reputation, as per the same English rhyme that states, "If in October you do marry / Love will come but riches tarry." (But who needs money when you've got each other?) Kabbalists find the four days between Yom Kippur and Sukkot (which may stretch into November) auspicious because they are associated with the four letters of the Tetragrammaton, which spell God's name in Hebrew. And there is something numerically satisfying about the idea that the tenth month of the year will ensure your marriage is a perfect 10.

NOVEMBER and **DECEMBER** generally bring risky weather. But the bad climate is associated with good luck in that same English rhyme, which promises, "If you wed in bleak November / Only joy will come, remember" and "When December's snows fall fast / Marry, and true love will last." Jews consider the month of Kislev, which corresponds with the second half of November and first half of December, extremely auspicious because it ends with Hanukkah, the miraculous Festival of Lights. Plus, the holidays are a good time to remember what you're thankful for—like true love.

MOON GAZING

Instead of considering the name at the top of the calendar page, you might look to the phases of the moon. Because the Jewish calendar is a lunar one, Jews consider the new moon, Rosh Chodesh ("the head of the month"), a blessed time that is ideal for new beginnings—giving you twelve lucky dates to choose from, or thirteen in a Jewish calendar leap year. The ancient Greeks preferred to wed during a waxing moon (rather than a waning one) so that the couple's joy and prosperity would continue

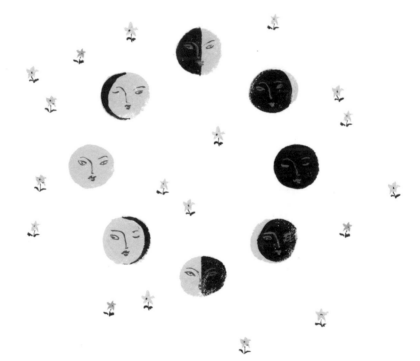

to grow. Similarly, in Holland and other countries, it's believed that the best time to marry is when the tide is rising, as the couple's fortunes will keep rising as well—something to keep in mind especially if you're having a seaside wedding. Whatever the phase of the moon during your wedding, it's a beautiful motif to use, since you're over the moon for each other. And if you are making it official during the second-in-one-month full moon known as blue, which takes place every three years or so, you can play up the fact that yours is a love that happens once in a blue moon.

IT'S YOUR LUCKY DAY

Although most weddings nowadays happen on weekends, that wasn't always the case—and Saturday isn't the luckiest day of the week to get married, folklorically speaking. In fact, it's the opposite according to this old English rhyme in *Every Woman's Encyclopaedia*: "Monday for wealth, Tuesday for health, Wednesday the best day of all, Thursday for losses, Friday for crosses, and Saturday no luck at all." (Sunday is not mentioned at all because it was considered a day for churchgoing, not wedding parties.)

In Judaism, Tuesday is considered auspicious for weddings because twice in the book of Genesis it is written that on the third day after Creation (that's right, a Tuesday), God looked around and "saw that it was good." On the other hand, Greeks consider Tuesdays unlucky, because Constantinople fell on a Tuesday—and Tuesday the 13th is the unluckiest of them all (see page 33).

An Italian proverb mandates that you shouldn't marry, travel, or begin a project on a Tuesday or a Friday. It doesn't go into why Tuesdays are bad, but the day Jesus died was a Friday.

Each day in *rokuyo*, the ancient Japanese six-day week, is associated with good or bad luck, with the day *taian*, which means "great peace" being the best for weddings, and the day *tomobiki,* or "pulling friends," the second best, except at the unlucky hour of noon, so the happy couple can draw their friends into the joy of their love. Today, Japan uses a seven-day week, but many calendars still include notations about rokuyo.

On a practical note, if you're looking to trim your wedding budget, a midweek day might be your lucky break—vendors and venues often discount their weekend rates by up to 20 percent.

BY THE NUMBERS

The actual digits in your wedding date can maximize good luck and counteract any negativity your month or day might bring. You can decide any number is personally your lucky one (because it's your birthday or was on the back of the football jersey you were wearing when you first met). But plenty of numbers hold the weight of centuries of cultural belief.

The number 2 signifies coupling up and living in harmony, which is why decorative scrolls and other accessories, such as candlesticks, are always displayed in pairs in Asia.

Meanwhile, in China, where the number 4 (*sei*) sounds like the Cantonese word for death, *séi,* buildings often skip the fourth floor.

Many East Asian cultures seek out the numbers 8 and 9 because of their homonyms—the word for eight (*baat*) sounds like "prosperity" (*faat*), and the word for nine (*gáu*), "long-lasting," (*gau*) in Cantonese. The relationship is very similar in Mandarin, too. And your luck is doubled if you bring the month into it, as well, getting married on August 8 or September 9, for example. Another bonus to the number 8: it looks like an infinity symbol tipped upright. When dealing with digits, remember that there are two sides to every story. Indian numerologists think the number

8 brings bad luck, some say because it curves up and down, promising a karmic roller coaster.

Several cultures suffer from triskaidekaphobia, a fear of the number 13, perhaps because it's the total of guests assembled at the Last Supper. But it's a lucky number in Judaism because there are thirteen books in the Torah, and it's the year when a child reaches the age of reason as a bar or bat mitzvah.

Another lucky number for Jews is 18. This is because every Hebrew letter has a numerical value; the letter heth is 8 and the letter yod is 10, and together they spell the word *chai,* or "life." On a celebratory occasion, you may stuff a gift envelope with sums of money ending in $18, or, even better, $36—double chai—and so on. In a romantic coincidence, 18 is also what you get if you add the numerical value of the word *ohavi,* or "beloved," spelled aleph (1), he (5), beth (2), and yod (10).

In Italy, 17 is unlucky because its Roman numeral depiction, XVII, can be scrambled into VIXI, the Latin word for "he lived," which appears on many a Roman gravestone. And according to La Smorfia, the Neapolitan dream-interpretation code, the number 17 signals misfortune. In addition, several cultures, including the Italians, interpret the assertion in Genesis that the biblical flood Noah and his family and menagerie— but nobody else—survived began on "the seventeenth day of the second month" of the year Noah was 600 to mean that it started on February 17. Of course, since 17 is a two-digit number, you could look at it as the sum of its parts (1 + 7 = 8), and argue that bad luck in Italy adds up to good luck in China.

TIMING IS
EVERYTHING

A long-held belief that exists in places from China to Chicago is that a couple should marry on the "upswing of the clock," when the hour, minute, and second hand are moving upward. Technically, this could be any time between 6:31 and 11:59 a.m. or p.m. The custom has evolved into the belief that weddings should take place on the half hour so that at least one of the hands is moving upward, and funerals on the hour. The reasoning is the same as with the waxing moon (see pages 30–31)—moving upward on the clock is associated with increasing joy and prosperity rather than diminishing returns.

CALL IN THE EXPERTS

Couture isn't only for fashion. Just as you can have a gown or tux custom-made for your wedding, you can have a date chosen to suit you to your best advantage. In several cultures, it is common practice for a couple to consult an astrologer or numerologist to pick the wedding date, or to make alterations if an already-chosen date is not ideal. For Hindu pairs, the date is selected according to Vedic astrology. The family astrologer consults the couple's birth dates and looks at the calendar and the *pan-changram,* or astrological almanac. If you're short on family astrologers, or prefer a more DIY approach, search "muhurat calculator" online and type in your info; the website will spit out a *muhurat,* or auspicious time for your ceremony to start. Should your astrologer (or website) tell you

you're *manglik,* or born under an unlucky astrological circumstance for marriage, you can get rid of that bad mojo by having a pandit, a Hindu priest, marry you to a clay pot, a doll, or a tree in a ceremony called a *kumbh vivah* (literally a "wedding with a pot"). This way, all of the negative energy is used up in your first "marriage," and your union to a human will be much happier.

East Asian culture gives similar analysis to a couple's Chinese zodiac signs, the Chinese calendar, and the astrological implications of the projected wedding date and time. Most Chinese almanac calendars have all the helpful info in one spot: the Gregorian calendar, the Chinese calendar, feng shui (see below), and astrological notations indicating whether or not a given day is good for "joyous events." A number of Chinese calendar apps let you plug in your info and give you a list of auspicious dates, but for highly personal service, consult a feng-shui master or fortune-teller.

SET A SENSE OF PLACE

When to wed gets the vast majority of superstitious attention, with convenience and preference dictating where to get hitched. But that doesn't have to be the case. Choose a place that has brought you luck: the congregation you grew up in, the college campus where you met, the restaurant where you went on your first date, or the country you visited on an important trip together. If guests get to see a place you love, chances are they'll enjoy it, too—and feel lucky to be there.

If your locale has no particular significance, but you still want your venue to bring some good juju, turn to feng shui, the ancient Chinese belief system about spaces and the energy that flows through them (or gets blocked, causing all kinds of trouble). The term *feng shui* means

"wind-water," and the philosophy suggests looking to natural elements to promote positive energy. Water brings peace; a riverfront, beach, or lakeside location is great, but a fountain works, too (if you have any belligerent guests, seat them facing the water, as it will calm them). In Java, some Muslim couples choose to hold their weddings near water-spouting statues because the flowing water symbolizes the continuing love the parents of the couple have for their children.

Gardens are also calming and create serene ambience. If you're getting married inside, you can rely on flowers or potted trees to bring

harmony—just avoid thorny plants such as cacti. To double down on your luck, choose auspicious flora (see pages 91–95).

Indoors, bright light heralds a bright future; aim for natural or side lighting instead of the harsh, overhead kind. If your space is windowless, decorate with mirrors, silver, and crystal to reflect any light.

You can use feng shui to create a harmonious mood in any space as long as you balance all five elements: water, wood (plants count), fire (artificial light or candles work, too), earth (minerals such as quartz fit the bill), and metal (think planters, silverware, and other decorative details).

If there's one universal fear for brides, it's rain, especially rain ruining an outdoor wedding. Doing what you can to shift fate, and the weather, in your favor, can help ease your worries. First, accept Murphy's Law, which states "Everything that can go wrong will." Outsmart Murphy by planning for things to go wrong so that they go exactly right. If you're having an outdoor wedding, make sure there's an indoor option, or buy a bunch of golf umbrellas and put down a deposit on a tent—better to spend money on shelter you won't end up needing than to be scrambling looking for options on a rainy wedding morning.

But how can you make things go right? In the American South, it's believed that burying an unopened bottle of bourbon upside down at the site of a wedding will guarantee good weather on the day of. No one is exactly sure why—although one theory holds that it's because everyone, including Mother Nature, loves bourbon, and the buried bottle is an offering that will please Her. Some couples do this exactly one month prior to the wedding, following the advice of this Southern ditty: "Bury a bottle of bourbon a month to the day in order to keep the rain away." Others perform the interment the morning of the wedding (and have their photographer capture the moment). And while some pairs leave the bottle buried, many dig it up post-vows to toast the good weather with their attendants.

In Ireland, those planning a wedding have a direct line to the powers that be courtesy of the Child of Prague, a sixteenth-century statue of Jesus as a child found in the Carmelite Church of Our Lady Victorious in Prague. Pope Pius X established the Czech church as a shrine in 1913, and after that, replicas of the Child of Prague became popular in Ireland where good-wedding-weather seekers either bury the statue in their yards or display it in a window of their home, facing out to keep an eye on the elements. This tradition has been practiced by Irish presidents, James Bond–star Pierce Brosnan, and even resort owners who wanted good weather for the G8 Summit in 2013.

Similarly, Catholics in the northern United States and Canada may hang their rosary beads outdoors—on a lamppost, bush, or clothesline—either the night before or the morning of the wedding while praying for good weather.

If all else fails, adjust your attitude. Okay, so the Irish believe that rain on a wedding day foretells a tearful marriage . . . but maybe they'll be tears of joy! And consider the Italian saying, "*Sposa bagnata, sposa fortunata*," which promises that a drenched bride will be a lucky bride, and the French "*Mariage pluvieux, mariage heureux*," which translates to "a rainy wedding means a happy marriage." In many other European countries, rain is associated with a bountiful harvest and is thought to bless brides with fertility. Hindus, who tie thread around the bride and groom's wrists during their ceremonies, say rain is fortunate because a wet knot is harder to untie. And American platitudes include the ideas that a wet day means good wishes are raining down on the couple and washing any troubles away, wedding day rain saves the bride from shedding any tears in her marriage, and drops hitting the bride's veil are especially auspicious (a variation on that: if it rains on your attendants, one of them will marry soon).

CHAPTER THREE

YOUR ENTOURAGE

Surround Yourself with Luck

You and your spouse-to-be are the key players in this whole she-bang. But it's your families, friends, attendants, and guests who make the day a wedding—without them, it would really just be an elopement. Your loved ones provide support for you as you take this major step in your life, and they demonstrate that even though you're pairing up as couple, you'll always be part of a larger community. The traditional roles played by your wedding party aren't only conventions of society; they're also reminders of where you've been and examples of where you're headed. These are the people who make you lucky. And they're devoting this day or night of their own lives to bringing you so much love and good fortune. Here's how you can make even more meaningful memories together.

AUSPICIOUS ATTENDANTS

Whether you have one attendant or ten, your best man is a best woman, your bridesmaids are bromaids, and your ring bearer is your dog, you want to spend your wedding day with the people who make you feel fortunate.

The Best Man and Groomsmen

The need for a designated sidekick is both practical and psychological. It was thought that if the groom needed to go back for something once he had left for the ceremony, he might turn his back on the marriage, too. Therefore, he needed a gofer to fetch anything he forgot. The best man is also a holdover from when weddings involved kidnapping the bride and the groom would recruit his pal who was best with a sword to help seize his intended. Groomsmen safeguarded the bride on her way to the wedding, protecting her from spurned suitors, angry family members, and anyone else who might stop the ceremony—which is why we have processionals and groomsmen dressed like the groom to confuse jealous rivals for the bride's affection.

Today, before the ceremony, the best man and groomsmen help the groom get ready. In Greece, preparations are ritualized with the *koumbaro* (see page 44), shaving the groom to demonstrate the trust between them. In some parts of Scotland, particularly in Fife, grooms still undergo a jokey foot-washing ritual, an old custom in which the groom's feet are smeared with grease and soot or ashes before being washed. The tradition is meant to gently mock the groom and bring him good fortune, as coal was considered lucky, but it also gives new meaning to the phrase "cold feet." The foot-washing may be an abridged version of "blackening the groom," another Scottish custom in which friends cover the groom in ashes, flour, treacle, and feathers and take him to pubs as part of his stag night.

In most Western cultures, at the end of the ceremony, the best man tips the officiant; according to American lore, it's lucky to do so with an odd sum of money, perhaps because even numbers can be divided by two, and the couple should be indivisible. Finally, at the reception, he toasts the couple, and the clinking of glasses scares off evil spirits.

The Maid or Matron of Honor and Bridesmaids

The very existence of bridesmaids is a testimony to seeking out good luck and avoiding bad. In ancient Rome, their purpose was to dress like the bride, thereby serving as a decoy for any evil spirits that might swoop in to steal her. They carried bouquets to resemble the bride and in homage to nature— a holdover from ancient Greece, where celebrants at religious ceremonies wore floral crowns to show their respect for the gods (see page 97).

Today, brides no longer need decoys, but they still appreciate the support bridesmaids bring while getting ready. In Scotland, the bride has her feet washed—without any ash or other muck—by a happily married friend, to get her marriage off on the right foot.

Other Attendants

The supporting cast at a wedding doesn't always stop at—or include— groomsmen and bridesmaids. Many cultures have honor attendants who perform an integral role in the ritual. In Greek Orthodox weddings, the couple appoint spiritual godparents to their marriage, known as the *koumbaro* and *koumbara*. They cross the wedding crowns over the bride and groom's heads and assist the priest in the ring exchange—actions believed to bring good luck to whomever performs them. (In other Orthodox Christian traditions, including Russian and Serbian, the priest performs the crowning. For more information on this ritual, see page 97.)

In Hispanic cultures, couples often name godparents in charge of certain wedding rituals, namely the *padrino* or *madrina de arras* (godfather or godmother of the coins) and *padrino* or *madrina de lazo* (godfather or godmother of the rope). The *arras* are thirteen coins said to bring the newlyweds prosperity, and the *lazo* is the unity cord that binds the couple together (see page 111). In both cases, the godparent will carry the ritual object down the aisle prior to the ceremony.

Lucky Littles

You don't need to be a folklorist to understand the symbolism of a flower girl—a tiny version of the bride who precedes her down the aisle. She is a visual reminder that the woman getting married was once a girl, and that she may soon have children of her own. What the flower girl carries can be significant as well. In ancient Rome, flower girls held sheaves of wheat, to represent fertility and abundance. In the Middle Ages, and as late as the middle of the last century, they toted garlic and dill to repel evil spirits (and maybe the plague, too). Elizabethan flower girls carried a silver chalice known as a "bride's cup." Today these little ladies may scatter petals from a basket, hold floral wreaths, or wave a flower-topped wand. Whatever type of flowers (or herbs) she throws, they're meant to line the couple's path with prosperity, fertility, and luck.

Traditionally, the ring bearer is the boy who carries the wedding bands down the aisle. Similar in role to the flower girl, he's a visual representation of the groom's past, and of the children the couple may have. In Filipino weddings, instead of having an adult *padrino* or *madrina de arras,* a couple will choose a child *arrhae* bearer to carry the coins.

If you or your spouse-to-be already has a child or children, they're sharing in your luck on your wedding day. They may love the idea of walking in the processional or being involved in one of the rituals, such as exchanging a family medallion along with the rings (see page 117). Or they may prefer to sit with their cousins and not worry about all the grown-ups looking at them. You'll all feel most fortunate if you follow their lead as to how they want to be incorporated into your ceremony.

As for mini guests, many couples opt for a child-free wedding. But remember that the noise of a baby crying at your ceremony is considered good luck, inviting more of that sound into your future.

KEEP YOUR LOVED ONES CLOSE

No matter how delighted you are to be getting married, it can be hard to feel lucky if one or more of the people you love most aren't present. A ritual can help you carry an absent loved one in your heart. The bride might hold a bouquet that looks like the one her late grandmother carried, is made up of her departed aunt's favorite blooms, or is wrapped in her late father's handkerchief. Or you might display the wedding photos of couples who came before you at the reception to make it feel a bit more like they're at the party.

While you're at it, make those people who *are* with you on the day feel lucky by acknowledging them in some way. Give corsages to your mother, mother-in-law, aunts, babysitters, first-grade teachers, or anyone who made something bloom in your heart. Do the same for gents with boutonnieres that have personal meaning—such as fishing flies for the uncle who always took you out on the lake.

After the bride and groom themselves, the parents of the couple are often the most involved in the wedding. They deserve special recognition for having raised the newlyweds-to-be and having helped them reach this milestone. The Khmer in Cambodia have a specific ritual for expressing filial gratitude: *bang chhat madaiy,* which means "holding umbrellas over parents." The couple do just that during a religious ceremony to indicate that now *they* are the ones who will provide shelter. While most other cultures don't have a ceremony to thank the parents, a simple gesture such as writing a card goes a long way.

PAY IT FORWARD

Several customs have evolved around the idea of the couple passing on their luck in love to unmarried friends—and none involve asking single-tons to shimmy to Beyoncé. Here are a few discreet ways to share the love.

TOSS THE BOUQUET (OR THE HAT. OR THE BREAD.) The bouquet toss, in which the bride throws her flowers over her shoulder to the waiting single women at the end of the reception, is meant to tag the next runner in the relay of marriage. This tradition is believed to have started in fourteenth-century France, and has seen several variations along the way. Queen Victoria gave each of her attendants a myrtle cutting from her bouquet instead of tossing the whole thing to one person. Nineteenth-century American brides threw a small nosegay to each of the maids—whoever got the one with a ring inside was said to be next. All iterations of the custom stem from the belief that the flowers in the bride's bouquet bring luck. With that as your starting point, you can use your creativity to decide how you will share your good fortune.

You don't, necessarily, have to throw flowers. In Poland, the bride tosses the *czepek,* or "marriage cap," she wears during the reception, while the groom lobs his tie at his single friends (see page 68). In parts of Greece, the bride throws a loaf of special wedding bread behind her toward her single friends; the one who catches it will be the next to marry (and anyone who's feeling peckish is in luck, too, as the bread is sliced, shared, and eaten). The ornately decorated bread is made with wheat (see pages 53 and 138), to symbolize fertility, and often shaped like a circle, to reference eternal love.

TOSS THE GARTER Sometimes practiced as a counterpoint to throwing the bouquet, the garter toss involves the groom removing a ceremonial garter from the bride's leg and throwing it to the assembled single men—the one who catches it then places it on the leg of the woman who caught the bouquet. It's meant to be auspicious for the people involved (because, much like the bouquet-snagger, the garter-catcher will marry next), but how lucky the winners feel depends on how comfortable they are with a room full of people watching one of them root around under the other's skirt. That may sound a little dicey, but it's positively restrained when you consider the origins of the custom. In Europe in the Middle Ages, people would tear off a piece of the bride's gown to keep as a lucky talisman (either at the altar, or after having followed the couple to the bedroom where the marriage would be consummated). Since this practice often resulted in the bride getting trampled, it evolved to her giving away the garters that held up her stockings to pacify luck-hungry guests.

PASS THE CROWN At a traditional Finnish wedding, the bride wears a golden crown, or *kruunumorsian,* with her veil. Post-ceremony, the single women blindfold the bride, form a circle around her, and dance until she manages to place her crown on one of their heads. Whoever is crowned is believed to be the next to marry.

TAG YOUR SOLE SISTERS While dressing for her wedding, a Greek or Turkish bride will invite friends looking for love to write their names on the soles of her shoes. Those whose names rub off by the time the bride is done dancing all night will marry next.

CHARM YOUR BRIDESMAIDS In the American South, brides spread luck to their bridesmaids by working divination into dessert, allowing them to have their fate and eat it, too. Charms on ribbons are hidden in the bottom layer of the wedding cake, and each bridesmaid tugs one prior to the cutting. Each "cake-pull" charm relates to a specific fortune: a sailboat or airplane means that 'maid will take a trip, a baby carriage predicts she'll become a mom, and so on. (Feel free to make up your own meanings for charms: a camera means she'll become an Instagram star, a typewriter indicates her novel will be published.) You needn't limit the fun to bridesmaids. Consider having a cake at the center of each table, a pull for every guest, and a card explaining the meaning of each.

CHAPTER FOUR

PARTY ON

The Celebrations Before the Celebration

There is vast cultural (and magical) precedent for having many, many parties as part of your nuptials. If you and yours have the stamina, a wedding weekend can be preceded by a wedding season, or even an entire wedding year. And no, you don't have to be the one in charge of planning all of these bashes. There's folkloric authority for family, friends, and anyone who loves the couple to host. Here are a few auspicious options for partying all engagement long.

SAY IT WITH SHOWERS

According to one legend, the custom of showering the bride with gifts arose in Holland in the seventeenth century when a father refused to give his daughter a dowry because he disapproved of her fiancé, a poor young miller. Instead, the thoughtful villagers threw her a party and brought her gifts to set up her new home. A whole bunch of presents is enough to make you feel lucky, but a shower also comes with superstitions revolving around the centerpiece of this party: the bride opening her gifts. Some hosts refuse to let the bride use scissors or a knife at all, which can make unwrapping dozens of boxes a challenge. That's because cutting symbolizes the end of a relationship in cultures from Italy to Argentina to the

United States. However, as the bride does get into her packages at showers in the States, it's said that the number of ribbons she tears represents the number of children she'll have. The ribbons are collected by a bridesmaid or friend and crafted into a "bow-quet" the bride will carry during her rehearsal or a hat she wears for the rest of the shower.

Not into all that unwrapping? Back in the day, a Finnish bride would knock on guests' doors and collect gifts in a pillowcase (see page 55).

It's said that whichever gift a bride opens first is the one she should use first to bring luck to her home. But if she unwraps a set of knives, she should "pay" the giver for it with a penny to prevent cutting off the friendship.

SO LONG, SINGLE LIFE

Ancient Spartans came up with the custom of getting all the guys together the night before the wedding to fête the groom and send him off to a fortunate future, which we now recognize as a bachelor party. Today, women have bachelorette equivalents, and some couples opt for co-ed parties. The Germans have a word for a co-ed bash—and that's meant literally. *Polterabend,* or "noisy evening," takes place the night before the wedding when guests bearing pottery meet the couple in front of the bride's family's home. Everyone smashes the ceramics, scaring away evil spirits. The engaged pair then cleans up the shards—a task meant to earn them a happy life together—and everyone parties on.

Things also get a little noisy in Scotland, where the bride's friends dress her in an odd getup and parade her through town as they bang pots, attracting customers to buy kisses from her by throwing money into the vessels. The groom also sports a humiliating costume, but he heads to bars with his friends, who sometimes then strip him and drop him off in front of his home.

In England and the United States, bachelor parties are called "stag nights," and in Australia, "buck nights," which brings a little luck to the equation, as deer, in China, are a symbol of longevity and prosperity. In Ireland and elsewhere in the United Kingdom, bachelorette festivities are called "hen parties," because they're a gathering of chicks. The name also happens to fit in with the Korean use of a hen and rooster to represent the bride and groom and bring luck to a wedding table (see page 82).

AUSPICIOUS ACTIONS

Aside from these two classic parties leading up to the main event, there are several other interactive things you can do to invite luck to your pre-wedding celebrations.

Bake Some Bread

The Thursday before a Bulgarian wedding, the bride, her mother, and other female friends and relatives knead *pitka*, or "butter bread"; the rising of the dough symbolizes the growth of a new family. The bread is baked and later served at the wedding, where the newlyweds tear the loaf in a wishbone-like contest to see who will have the upper hand in their marriage, before distributing it to their guests.

Drum It Out

Muslims may have one *dholki* or several in the week or two leading up to the wedding. The word means "drum" because one is played, as friends and relatives of the bride and groom sing, dance, and feast. Either the groom's or the bride's family (or both!) can throw a *dholki*.

Have a Good Cry

Among the Tujia community in parts of China, it's considered lucky for the bride—then her female relatives—to sob leading up to the wedding. The theory is that if she's sad ahead of time, she'll be happy in her married life, but the practice also enables her to express her sorrow at leaving her family and vice versa. A month before the wedding, the bride will sit in the hall for an hour a day and perform the "Crying Wedding Song." One week in, her mom joins her, then come her grandmother and any sisters, and it becomes a big old pity party.

Give Them a Hand

Several days prior to Sikh weddings, both families get together, each at their own home, for a *maiya* purification ceremony, which involves rubbing turmeric paste, called *vatna,* on the bride's and groom's hands, legs, feet, arms, and faces, and tying lucky red strings around their wrists. It gets messy and hilarious and, at the end, the mothers of the bride and groom each make three *vatna* handprints on the outside wall of their houses, to share their joy by indicating to passers-by that there is a wedding in the family.

Make Your Bed

In some countries, the couple's loved ones oversee the making of their marital bed, to bless them with fertility and prosperity. Called *Au Chuang,* or "setting up the bed" in China, this ritual is held on an auspicious date three days to a week before the wedding, when a happily married woman with children makes up the bed in lucky red sheets and covers it with fruit and red envelopes holding monetary gifts in sums that end in the fortunate number 9. Then children jump on the bed to invite progeny.

In Greece, the sheets aren't red but the idea is the same—only it's unmarried women who race to make up the bed, and whomever fits the last pillow into a pillowcase is said to marry next. Friends and relatives cover the bed in gold coins and paper money (for wealth), rose petals (for love), rice (for fertility), and Jordan almonds (for a sweet life) before babies are placed on top and children jump on the bed in the gender order the couple request. In both countries, the bed remains untouched until the wedding.

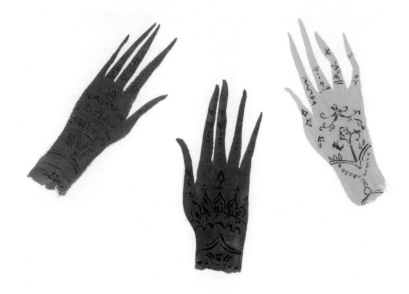

Paint the Town

All over South Asia (among both Hindus and Muslims), in the Middle East, and among Swahili communities in Kenya and Sephardic Jews worldwide, brides are adorned with *mehndi,* henna designs painted on their hands and up their forearms. With their reddish color, these patterns invite luck and fertility, repel the evil eye (see page 89), and add to the bride's beauty. While the bride's mehndi is the most ornate and extensive—the couple's initials may be hidden in the intricate patterns for the groom to find later—her female relatives and friends also wear mehndi as a means of joining in the celebration, often having it applied by makeup artists at a ladies-only party. Sephardic Jewish henna parties are co-ed, and are considered the moment when the bride joins the groom's family. They also include a presentation of seven baskets of gifts to the bride, including Jordan almonds (see page 151), sheets, perfume, and jewelry.

THE LAST SUPPER

In the United States, it's traditional for the groom's family to host the rehearsal dinner, a night-before party for the families and attendants, and perhaps all out-of-town guests, right after the rehearsal where every one practices their role in the wedding ceremony. But that's not your only option! In Guyana, the couple's families get together at a *queh queh,* a lavish celebratory meal and dance-off where relatives sing songs, make jokes at the lovebirds' expense, offer matrimonial advice, and ask the pair to "show me your science." In response, the couple perform a sexy dance that indicates they know what to do to create future generations.

In Ireland up through the early-twentieth century, the bride's family served the groom a goose dinner the night before the wedding, or as soon as the couple's engagement was confirmed. The bird was a prelude to the signing of complex documents called "The Bindings," which stipulated how the couple would live, right down to how often they would take their parents and in-laws to Sunday mass. After those papers were signed, it was believed that the wedding was as good as done, which led to the expression, "his goose is cooked." Today the ritual, called Aitin' the Gander, is just an excuse for a nice meal.

Music may be the food of love, according to Shakespeare, and it's definitely the inspiration for Indian couples' rehearsal dinners. The night before the wedding, guests attend the *sangeet* (the Sanskrit word for music), a party where the bride's and groom's friends and family members dance, sing, and perform skits to entertain the couple. Even if you haven't brushed up on your Bollywood moves, a dance party/sing-a-long makes a raucous rehearsal dinner alternative that encourages mingling between families and old and new friends.

PRE-VOW PRACTICES

Some events are so linked to the wedding they take place immediately before the ceremony begins. A long-held, cross-cultural belief is that it's bad luck for the groom to see the bride—or her dress—before the wedding. This may have stemmed from arranged marriages, and the fear that once the groom saw his intended, he would take an instant dislike to her and change his mind.

Today, while many couples enjoy the drama of the groom getting a vision of his bride for the first time as she walks down the aisle, others don't like missing cocktail hour to pose for portraits. Photographers came up with a work-around in order to take pictures before the ceremony without inviting bad luck: the "first look" is just that—a moment set up by and for the camera, when the bride and groom see each other in their wedding finery for the first time before the ceremony begins.

Just before the ceremony itself, observant Jewish grooms will celebrate with the groomsmen at a *tisch* (the Yiddish word for table). The guys eat, drink, and (gently) heckle the groom as he tries to display his erudition by giving a speech. While the men are making merry, the bride sits on a throne like a queen, entertained by her ladies as they dance for her while music plays. The gender-segregated gatherings end when the groom and his friends dance over to the bride's party for the signing of the ketubah (the marriage contract). Next comes the *bedeken,* or "veiling," in which the groom lifts the bride's veil to see her face, then replaces it, ensuring he is marrying the woman he proposed to, and not getting the old switcheroo, as in the biblical story of Rachel and Leah. Today, some Jewish couples open their pre-vow gatherings to friends of either gender. Others prefer to be led to each other backward before they turn and see that the other person is, in fact, their intended, in a gender-neutral "veiling," but with no veils required.

In India, a rousing game of *joota chupai,* or "stealing the shoes," is played before, during, and immediately after the ceremony. When the groom takes off his ornate slippers before stepping onto the platform where the ritual will take place, one of the bride's relatives grabs them and ferrets them away to an undisclosed location. His relatives try to steal them back or discover their hiding place as the long ceremony continues. Once it's over and he needs his shoes to leave, he has to pay a ransom to get them back. It's all done with a playful attitude meant to kick off a lifetime of both families celebrating together.

Whatever your religion, a few pre-vow drinks, songs, and laughs with friends and family can help you relax and focus on the joyous ceremony ahead, instead of sweating the small stuff.

CHAPTER FIVE

CLOTHES
ENCOUNTERS

Ensembles for the Entire Wedding Party

Wedding clothes are inherently magical. They have the power to transform—witness the entire genre of TV shows devoted to a woman trying on wedding gowns, waiting for the moment when she slips into the right one and suddenly becomes a *bride*. It's not just the bride's gown (and veil and shoes and jewelry) that is weighted with cultural meaning. Beliefs and rituals are associated with what the groom and attendants wear, too. Not to mention the accessories the main players carry with them. Read on for ways to dress yourself— and everyone else—in good fortune.

COLOR OUTSIDE THE LINES

In the days before bridal boutiques, women were simply married in their best dress, which they could wear again and again throughout their marriage. Here's a rhyme from a nineteenth-century *Old Farmer's Almanac* about what the color of the bride's dress foretold:

Married in **White**, you have chosen right.

Married in **Grey**, you will go far away,

Married in **Black**, you will wish yourself back.

Married in **Red**, you will wish yourself dead.

Married in **Green**, ashamed to be seen.

Married in **Blue**, you will always be true.

Married in **Pearl**, you will live in a whirl.

Married in **Yellow**, ashamed of your fellow.

Married in **Brown**, you will live in the town.

Married in **Pink**, your spirit will sink.

Take these predictions with a grain of salt, or use them as inspiration to make up your own rhyme to justify the dress you have your heart set on—"Married in Blush, with happiness you'll be flush."

Keep in mind that certain colors do carry symbolic weight in various cultures. Read the following list to defend your choices to Aunt Sadie who is shocked that you don't plan to marry in white, or to your bridesmaids who wonder why you've chosen a shade that may not be their best look. And for color advice that extends beyond fashion to décor, see page 80.

WHITE It wasn't until Queen Victoria wed in white in 1840 (to match the lace she'd chosen for her gown), that alabaster wedding dresses became a trend. White gowns were a status symbol at first, as only the wealthy could afford a best dress in such an impractical color. But the shade quickly came to symbolize purity, becoming the de facto hue for brides. Victoria wasn't the first to wear white, though. In ancient Rome, brides were clad in white as a symbol of their joy. In Japan, as in much of Asia, white is the color of mourning, but a Shinto bride wears white for the ceremony, then changes to a silk kimono that incorporates both white and red, symbolizing the death of her old life and the beginning of her married life. Death and new life are also ever-present in the white wedding blanket of the Hopi bride, which the groom and his family make for her, and which she wears at her wedding, dons once a year for the annual Kachina Festival, and is wrapped in when she dies (when it becomes a cloud that transports her to the underworld). Each of the blanket's four corners has colorful tassels woven with fertility symbols.

BLUE After white, blue is the color most linked to weddings, as it has long symbolized fidelity. (Just think of the "something blue" rhyme—see page 77.) In biblical times, Jewish brides had blue ribbons sewn onto their wedding dresses to show loyalty and modesty. It's also a lucky color for Christian brides because it's associated with the Virgin Mary, who is often shown in ecclesiastical art wearing the shade both because it recalls heaven and because blue paint, once made of lapis lazuli, was the most precious pigment.

BLACK In previous centuries, some Spanish brides wore black to show that they'd be devoted to their spouses until they died. (Morbid or romantic? Or a little of both?) In the United States, where traditionally black has been reserved for funerals, it was once considered rude to wear black to a wedding, as if the event had thrown you into mourning. But today, the color is associated with formality and sophistication (as in black-tie), and is now a popular option for bridesmaids' dresses and even bridal gowns.

BROWN Perhaps the most traditional versions of brown wedding attire come from Fiji and Samoa, where the couple's clothes are made of tapa, cloth crafted from mulberry tree bark (which veers toward beige), and decorated with black, brown, and white patterns that have regional significance. The designs were originally made with soil and clay, and the cloth is thought to be a fertility symbol, as it comes from the bark of a flowering tree (see page 86).

GREEN Korean brides traditionally wear a celadon *wonsam*, as green is a calming color in feng shui (see pages 35–37). Many Asian brides choose jade jewelry, which is considered very lucky, especially if it is a gift from a friend or relative who has worn the item herself and wishes to share her happiness. But Irish brides avoid green because it's the fairies' favorite color, and it's believed that if fairies happen upon a wedding, they'll lure the bride away. On the other hand, for the same reason, it's good luck for bridesmaids to wear green—to distract the mischievous sprites.

METALLIC While the number, color, and pattern of the outfits worn by Khmer couples in Cambodia varies, the most elaborate ensembles are gold silk to demonstrate that the bride and groom are equal to royalty on their wedding day. And in many places, the bride is covered in gold jewelry, as in Djibouti, where an Afar bride may shield her face in intricate gold chains that hang from her headpiece like a veil and attach to her nose ring, indicating the importance of the occasion.

PINK Fuchsia in Hindi is called *rani,* or "queen," because Indian queens historically wore the shade.

PURPLE Purple clothing is a symbol of power, passion, and prosperity, associated with royalty in ancient Rome, much of western Europe, and parts of Africa (maroon is one of the colors of ceremonial *aso-oke* cloth worn at weddings and by Yoruba chiefs). But it indicates mourning in the Catholic Church, where priests wear purple to say mass for the dead.

RED Many Indian brides wear red saris, as the color, associated with the rising sun, represents love, purity, fertility, the goddess Durga, and goddess worship in general. The bridal dress described in the Hindu sacred text *The Ramayana* is a gossamer red fabric embroidered with gold. Chinese brides also favor red, as it's the color of luck and wealth and is believed to drive away evil spirits. (A Chinese bride will often change clothes at least twice during her wedding, perhaps from a white, Western-style gown to a red *qipao* for the tea ceremony to a party dress for the reception.) Yemeni brides wear red onyx necklaces to repel the evil eye (see page 89).

YELLOW Brides wear yellow in parts of northern India, where it represents prosperity, perhaps because it's associated with good wheat and mustard harvests or because the color traditionally came from expensive saffron dye and was reserved for the wealthy or ceremonial occasions.

MULTIPLE COLORS In Elizabethan times, bridesmaids would tie colored ribbons into love knots that symbolized the bond between the couple and sew them onto the bride's dress. Each color represented a different virtue (blue for fidelity, for example). At the end of the party, the groomsmen and guests were invited to untie the bride's knots, which was said to pave the way for a pain-free childbirth down the road.

Korean brides who don't wear pale green choose floral robes with trailing sleeves embroidered in blue (for the earth), yellow (for mankind), and red (for heaven). The traditional Navajo bridal outfit is made up of four colors that honor the directions of the compass: black for the north, white for the east, blue for the south, and yellow for the west. In Swaziland, the beaded bridal apron is red for fertility, white for purity, and black for wealth.

The kente cloths that make up wedding attire for both bride and groom in Ghana contain colored stripes, including yellow for fertility, pink for feminine power, blue to evoke the heavens, and silver to represent the moon, the ultimate expression of female strength and beauty. Couples often wear matching kente cloths as a visual representation of their unity.

CROWNING GLORIES

Juliet caps had their moment (the 1970s), birdcage veils skew vintagey cool, tiaras are beloved by princess brides, and floral accessories will always pack boho appeal. But what tops a bride's wedding ensemble—and sometimes a groom's, too—isn't just trendy; it's also associated with luck in many cultures.

Veils

Brides have been wearing veils since antiquity. There are three auspicious reasons for the custom: First, to confuse or scare off evil spirits eager to harm the beautiful bride. Second, to make it harder for runaway brides to escape (some theorize that the veil represents the blanket a groom-abductor would throw over her head back when men kidnapped their brides). And third, to symbolize that the groom's love is beyond skin-deep—that he would marry her even if he could not see her radiant face.

Over her white gown, an ancient Roman bride was covered in a long, yellow-orange-red veil meant to deter evil spirits by tricking them into thinking she was on fire. Chinese brides wear red veils en route to their ceremonies, and some Turkish and Eastern European brides also wear red veils to block the evil eye (see pages 65 and 89), as the lucky color symbolizes blood and, therefore, life. If your veil or gown is trimmed in tassels, those are evil eye repellers, too (which is also why they're found on priestly garb and military uniforms in much of the Middle East).

A cross-cultural superstition posits it's lucky for a happily married woman to place the veil on the bride's head so her good fortune will rub off. Another widely held belief says that borrowing the veil of a happily married woman is auspicious, as you're borrowing some of her luck as well. In Armenian weddings, the maid of honor waves the veil above the bride's head three times for health, happiness, and prosperity, before passing it over the bridesmaids' heads to share the bride's luck in love.

A Latvian bride will wear her veil until midnight, then pass it on to whichever relative is likely to marry next, and put on a "marriage cap" that signifies she's now a wife, in a ritual called *mičošana,* or "the changing of the headdress." (The groom may represent his transition into a husband by putting on a Panama hat.) A similar ritual, the *oczepiny,* or "unveiling and capping ceremony," traditionally took place in Poland, where the removal of the veil and unbraiding of the bride's hair occurred at midnight, so that as one day transitioned into the next, she passed from girlhood into marriage. Her grandmother gave her the marriage cap, which she refused three times, reluctant to leave behind her youth, before accepting it. Today, the bride still removes her cap, but tosses it, bouquet-style. The groom does the same with his tie, and the singletons who catch each are said to be next to marry.

According to American custom, if a bride's veil is torn, it's good luck. If you're wearing a long veil, weighing down the edges by sewing coins into the hem helps to attract wealth and avoid wardrobe malfunctions.

Headpieces

Whether they're simple floral wreaths or ornate gold coronets, wedding crowns symbolize—as the Archbishop of Canterbury said at the marriage of Prince Charles and Lady Diana—that on their wedding day every couple is the king and queen of love.

In Orthodox Christian weddings, crowns, or *stefana* in Greek, are part of the religious service. The crowns, which can be made of flowers or precious metals and are tied to each other by a length of ribbon, are crossed above the bride and groom before being placed on their heads. A similar ritual occurs in a Thai ceremony, in which the couple's parents crown them with white fabric wreaths called *mongkol,* or "circles of luck," linked by a thread, before holy water is poured over their hands (see page 114).

Other cultures have crowns as part of their stylistic, if not religious, traditions. In Sweden, Norway, and Denmark, brides wear *brudkronan,* flared metal crowns that look like they came out of a fairy tale, as a symbol of virginity. In Finland, the crown, called a *kruunumorsian,* is gold and plays a starring role in a divination game to see which bridesmaid will marry next (see page 48).

In China, the bride wears a headband called a *fengguan,* or the "phoenix crown," as the proud bird is a bridal symbol (see page 83), and before he leaves for the ceremony, the groom takes part in the *jia guan,* or "capping ritual," in which his father places a hat adorned with cypress leaves on his head to show he is taking on the responsibility of a family. In many African countries, including Nigeria, a groom wears a *fila,* a cloth hat that stands up in crownlike fashion. Some Hindu and Muslim grooms wear turbans, a symbol of royalty and luck, and in northern India and parts of Bangladesh and Pakistan, a Hindu groom gets a veil of sorts, called a *sehara*: garlands of small flowers or beads are attached to his turban to shield his face and make him resemble the god Vishnu on his wedding day.

There are also veil and crown alternatives. A Shinto bride in Japan wears a *tsunokakushi,* a white silk headdress whose name means "horn hider," as it's said to conceal any metaphorical horns associated with jealousy or ego, and to help her become a good wife. A more bride-friendly theory holds that the horns hidden aren't the bride's, but those of jealous demons. In Nigeria, Yoruba brides top their ensembles with *Gele* headwraps, while Igbo brides wear auspicious red coral beads (symbols of joy and life) strung as headbands, caps, or crowns.

HAIR AND MAKEUP

In Europe during the Middle Ages, a bride wore her hair loose or braided to signal her status as a virgin. Even after that, Irish brides chose braids plaited with lace or ribbons, as symbols of femininity. A Yemeni bride wears thick braids to show fertility—if her hair isn't long enough, she'll add faux braids, sometimes made of wool, under an ornate headdress.

Today, many African brides have elaborately plaited hairstyles, and in some regions, the braids are covered in clay; the reddish color is thought to promote love. (Among the Masai, the groom rubs clay into his hair, too.) In China, the bride takes part in a *shang tou* hairdressing ritual in which a lucky woman—one whose parents, husband, and children are all living—helps coil the bride's hair into a bun while repeating blessings.

The night before the wedding is when lucky hairdressing rituals take place in Vietnam. The bride's mother brushes her daughter's hair using three combs, making a different wish for her with each one. Cambodian Khmer couples participate in a *gaat sah* hair-cutting ceremony just before the reception, when two singers dance around them, pretending to cut their hair to rid them of any baggage from their past.

Bridal makeup isn't as rich with symbolism as hair, but some cultures embrace auspicious face paint. To ward off evil spirits, a traditional Korean bride would wear *yonji konji,* three red circles of makeup (or paper), on her forehead and each cheek. Indian brides still wear *kajal,* kohl eyeliner, to ward off bad luck (and, as a bonus, define their eyes). And there's a Hindu ritual that brings hair and makeup together—the groom placing *sindoor,* vermilion powder, on the part of his bride's hair, a sign that she is a married woman. Traditionally, women applied sindoor to their parts daily until they were widowed, when it was wiped off as part of the mourning ritual.

IT'S ALL IN THE DETAILS

For both brides and grooms, wedding day accessories are an easy way to invite good fortune and ward off bad fortune.

Shoes

After the veil, shoes are the next best supporting accessory in a bride's wedding ensemble. Many modern bridal shoe designers incorporate blue in the design or sole of the shoe as a lucky "something" (see page 77), but there are auspicious customs you can adopt whatever shoes you're wearing. In Poland, traditionally, the bride's shoes have to be closed-toe so that good luck doesn't escape through an open front, while in Scandinavia, the bride may wear a silver coin from her dad in her left shoe and a gold one from her mom in her right, as a way of making sure she'll always have enough money in her married life. Among the Zuni Native Americans, it was once the groom's job to craft his bride-to-be's leather wedding boots as proof he could care for her.

In much of Eastern Europe and parts of Russia, the groom will drink a toast "out of the shoe" of the bride. (For the sake of hygiene, this usually involves wedging a champagne flute into the shoe.) During a Portuguese wedding reception, the bride may take off her shoes and place them on the dance floor. Guests wishing to dance with her put money inside to pay for the privilege, and the couple take that money to help fund their honeymoon. A Hindu groom's shoes get a lot of attention when the bride's family hides them in the traditional and hilarious *joota chupai* shoe-stealing ritual during the ceremony (see page 59). Hasidic Jews also focus their good luck on the groom's shoes: he's meant to untie any shoelaces (and his tie, and any other knotted pieces of clothing) to ensure a problem-free marriage. Similarly, in Syria, grooms of yore avoided wearing any kind of knot; doing so was said to cause impotence.

Jewelry

The most obvious way to have jewelry bring you luck on your wedding day is to wear an heirloom piece from someone you love, or something that has been worn by multiple brides in happy marriages, like your sisters, cousins, or aunts. But there are plenty of jewelry rituals to follow.

Once a couple are wed in India, each one of them wears a silver toe ring on the second toe of both of their feet to show that they're married. In some areas, the groom slips the ring on the bride's foot during the Hindu ceremony, before placing a *mangalsutra,* or holy thread, necklace around her neck as a symbol of their union. Each mangalsutra contains black beads meant to repel the evil eye (see page 89), and the groom may also hide a piece of iron in his pocket for the same purpose.

In Western cultures, superstition states that a bride should not wear pearls, as the ancient Greeks believed they were the tears of the gods, and wearing them would foretell a sad married life. But a competing superstition holds that pearls substitute for any tears the bride might have otherwise shed during her marriage, making them a good luck choice. And the ancient Greeks themselves felt that wearing pearls would prevent a bride from crying on her wedding day. In South Asia, a Hindu tale has Krishna picking a pearl from the ocean floor and giving it to his daughter, Pandaia, at her wedding. And the Koran describes pearls as one of the rewards awaiting the faithful in paradise.

Igbo brides wear coral bead necklaces, earrings, and/or crowns, as the red color symbolizes joy, life, and wealth, and the size and shape of the beads indicate the status of the wearer.

Among Native Americans, Hopi and Navajo brides wear squash blossom necklaces, which are traditional fertility symbols because of their resemblance to flowers—and, some say, to the end of a pomegranate— and because the beads leading up and down to the main pendant can be seen as the bride's future children surrounding her.

On the west coast of Africa, cowrie shells, which are thought to boost fertility, feature heavily in bridal jewelry.

Everything Else

Other accessories aren't necessarily must-haves, but they can be lucky nice-to-haves. Shawls are welcome at a winter wedding, especially if you're marrying a Scottish groom, who may wrap his family's clan tartan around your shoulders during the vow exchange for luck—and to match his kilt. Or you could choose a mirrored or sequined shawl inspired by the *handira,* Moroccan wedding blankets Berber brides wrap around them- selves after the ceremony, which their female relatives make for them, attaching metallic discs that sparkle and jingle to scare away evil spirits.

Gloves aren't necessarily worn by brides today, but in the Victorian era, a pair of them was the last thing the bride would put on, looking away

from the mirror so that she wouldn't see herself in her complete wedding attire before the ceremony. Traditionally, Greek brides would hide a sugar cube in one of the fingers of their gloves to ensure married life would be sweet.

Handkerchiefs are also now fairly rare in day to-day life, but they often see a revival at weddings. The bride may carry a handkerchief embroidered with blue thread for luck, or wrap her bouquet in one that belonged to a beloved family member. A Belgian bride will hold a handkerchief embroidered with her first name, which she'll later frame and hang on the wall in her home. When the next family wedding rolls around—be it her sister's or her daughter's—she takes down the frame, removes the handkerchief and has that bride-to-be's name embroidered on it so that the heirloom is passed on, along with the luck and love it represents. On the Greek island of Corfu, brides used to wear *tsoutsoumides,* red handkerchiefs printed with peacock feathers; today they're tied to the mirrors of the car transporting the bride, and are held by the bride and groom as they lead the wedding dance after the ceremony. An Irish bride may carry a handkerchief that she will eventually fashion into a christening bonnet for her first child—who will then turn it back into a "magic hankie" to carry on his or her wedding day.

When it comes to hankies, don't forget your loved ones. In Switzerland, attendants offer arriving guests lucky colored handkerchiefs, and receive a coin in return; the money goes to help the newlyweds set up their home. Or follow the Hungarian custom of the bride giving her spouse-to-be an auspicious number of handkerchiefs (three or seven, which are prime numbers that, like the couple, can't be divided).

Fans are seldom found rattling around in handbags these days, but they, too, live on at weddings. A Nigerian bride carries an *abebe,* or "hand fan," as the finishing touch of her engagement and wedding outfits to help her keep cool under all the aso-oke fabric. And a Chinese bride traditionally brought a fan with her when she left home for the wedding, dropping it en route to the groom's house to show she was leaving her old life behind.

Then there are the petticoat pockets where brides once hid objects. That might have been tiny scissors to cut the evil eye (see page 89), or, in early-American custom, a pouch with a dollar and bits of bread, wood, and cloth, to ensure the pair would always have money, food, a home, and clothing. Today, a bride may have a good-luck coin sewn into the lining of her dress, or her wedding date embroidered there in blue thread.

Of course, in Western cultures, the most commonly thought-of accessories are the ones that fulfill the old English rhyme "Something old, something new, something borrowed, and something blue." The something old is meant to indicate that the love the bride had before getting married will continue. The something new is to guarantee luck in her married life. Something borrowed is a reminder that her friends will always be there to help. (It's also said that if your something borrowed is on loan from a single woman, she will get engaged within the year.) And the something blue is for everlasting devotion and fidelity (see page 63).

There's a last, lesser-known line to that ditty: "And a sixpence in her shoe," in England, or "And a shiny penny in her shoe," in America. That symbolism is fairly obvious: a lucky coin to make sure the couple will always have money. A four-leaf clover is a softer substitute, though some say walking on the coin is meant to cause discomfort on the day to spare the bride a rocky road in her marriage. Variations on this custom include having the father of the bride give her the coin to pass good fortune down through the generations, or the groom give it to her to bring them both luck. Some say it's twice as auspicious if the coin has the bride's birth year on it. A new coin with your wedding year seems pretty fortunate, too! A coin from the currency of your or your betrothed's family's "old country" has significance as you'll be carrying part of your past into your future.

CHAPTER SIX

DIVINE DÉCOR

Deck Out Your Day

Y ou want your wedding to look lovely. Why not have it look lucky, too? Every opportunity for design or décor is a chance to work in a symbol that's understood to be auspicious, either universally or personally. Pick a color palette that invites joy, or choose hues that are significant for you as a couple—black, blue, and silver may recall the night sky on the camping trip during which you got engaged. Select a meaningful motif for your paper goods, or mail invitations with postage stamps showcasing a flower in your bouquet or picturing Billie Holiday, whose recording of "Come Rain or Come Shine" is your first dance song. Whatever your style, there's a symbol for you.

COLOR THEORY

Choosing a palette for your day ties the look together—and can also change its mood, according to feng shui (see pages 35–37). To customize your colors, consult a feng-shui website, book, or practitioner to find out what shades work best with your birth element (the material—wood, fire, earth, metal, or water—associated with your Chinese horoscope). For a taste, read through the feng-shui color primer below. (For the significance of hues in clothing specifically, see pages 63–66.)

BLACK AND WHITE When paired, these represent yin and yang, or female and male energies, and are therefore auspicious wedding colors. Also lucky together are black and green, which promote wealth and longevity, and black and purple, which bring prosperity and success.

BLUE AND GREEN Both of these seaside shades are considered calming, and green is also thought to inspire growth.

METALLICS Silver, gold, rose-gold, copper, brass, or pewter add formality and prosperity to a celebration because they look like precious metals. Plus, they are believed to promote creativity, fertility, and healing.

ORANGE Warming and energetic, orange is also the color of the marigolds used to make celebratory garlands in India, where saffron is an auspicious hue.

PURPLE When paired with white, purple brings harmony, and when matched with black, success.

RED The color of fire and lifeblood, red is energetic and bold. It represents male yang energy, and benefits from being balanced with its yin counterpart, pink.

YELLOW A color that brightens, yellow adds energy to your day. And yellow and white together symbolize heaven and earth.

FIRST MATES

If you like the idea of a mascot, find your wedding's spirit animal, whether it's a species that mates for life or part of a specific cultural tradition.

ALBATROSSES These big birds dance to show their love for each other, and are together until death do they part. Kind of like the two of you.

BALD EAGLES Independent, majestic, and patriotic, the national mascots of the United States migrate separately, but come together year after year.

BARN OWLS Symbols of wisdom, snowy-white barn owls are emblems of monogamy, too.

BEAVERS These industrious little fur balls are very homey, constructing dams and raising families in perfect harmony after pairing up for life.

BUTTERFLIES In China, butterflies are associated with longevity, because the Mandarin word for butterfly, *hu-tieh*, includes the word *tieh*, which means "seventy years." They're also symbols of love, as a legend about the ancient sage Zhuangzi holds that he chased a butterfly into a garden where he spotted a beautiful young woman and fell in love with her. In Japan, butterflies are said to represent the departed souls of beloved people. And for many cultures, butterflies signal transformation, the human soul, and our ability to change, because they begin as humble caterpillars.

CRANES These elegant birds are auspicious in Japan, where they're embroidered onto bridal kimonos, because they're said to live for a thousand years. Some couples fold *senbazuru*, one thousand origami cranes, with which to decorate their wedding. And Japanese fathers traditionally give sets of one thousand cranes to their daughters to use as décor on the big day. Today they're available from origami artists on handicraft sites such as Etsy.

DRAGONS In China, the dragon and the phoenix represent a married couple: the phoenix is the strongest symbol of female yin energy, and the dragon represents the male energy, yang.

DUCKS These monogamous fowl are a beloved nuptial symbol in Korea, where a pair of wooden "wedding ducks" were traditionally displayed on a table during ceremonies and are still a popular gift for newlyweds. Now they're mass-produced, but in the past they were carved by a woodworker blessed with the "five fortunes": wealth, health, a good wife, no divorced relatives, and multiple sons.

FRENCH ANGELFISH These sweet sea creatures swim side by side all their lives, and spin around each other in a love dance called "carouseling."

GIBBONS They may be cheeky monkeys, but they're also reliable partners for life.

HENS Along with "wedding ducks," a Korean nuptial table will hold figures of a hen and a rooster, symbolizing the bride and groom, in front of a screen of peonies.

LOVEBIRDS That name speaks for itself!

ORCAS Devoted mates until the end, black-and-white killer whales are also formally dressed in nature's tuxedo.

OTTERS These water mammals hold hands in their sleep so as not to float apart in the stream.

PENGUINS Monogamous during breeding season, many penguin pairs return to each other year after year. Plus, they're black-tie-ready.

PHOENIXES A bridal emblem in China, phoenixes are also beloved because of the Greek myth that they rise from the ashes, turning tragedy into triumph.

PRAIRIE VOLES These mammals don't just huddle together through long, Midwestern winters; they remain together until death do they part.

RED FOXES Even if you're not marrying a ginger, you've got to admire these foxy fauna, who mate for life.

SEAHORSES These underwater wonders wrap their tails around each other to stay close in the current.

SWANS Largely monogamous, swans are also beautiful and, when they swim up to each other, can form a heart shape with their long necks.

TURTLE DOVES It's hard to find a more classic symbol of marriage than these birds who bill and coo their whole lives long.

WOLVES Mates for life, they howl at the moon together. Forever.

NATURAL WONDERS

No one's a better decorator than Mother Nature. Several of her greatest hits have become meaningful symbols that could also be used to dress up your day.

CLOVERS Four-leaf clovers are lucky to the Irish, partly because they're rare (with shamrocks, the three-leaf variety, being easier to find) and because the leaves resemble hearts. Each one of the four leaves also represents a blessing: some say respect, wealth, love, and health, while others ascribe them to hope, faith, love, and luck. (For more symbolic plants, see pages 92–94.)

FIRE More than a few venues prohibit open flames for liability reasons (buzzkills!). If yours doesn't, consider candlelight, fireworks, sparklers, or a post-wedding bonfire for roasting s'mores. Not only does firelight symbolize warmth, hope, and divinity (Hindus call Agni, the fire god, "The Radiant One"), but also there's the cross-cultural idea of an eternal flame. This may have originated with the always-burning hearth at the Oracle of Delphi, but can just as easily represent the love burning in your hearts. For Zoroastrians, a physical flame represents the spiritual flame, *mainyu athra*, within each of us. In Japan, newlyweds may stop by every table at the reception to greet guests and light a candle, spreading a warm glow to the group.

MOONLIGHT Another natural phenomenon that is considered lucky (see pages 30–31), the moon is also associated with phrases such as being so in love you're "over the moon," or admiring someone so much you think they "hung the moon." A crescent moon had special significance in ancient Egypt, where it was linked

with Isis, the mother goddess, and was the sign of the Ottoman Empire, where it became an emblem atop many mosques. The center of a Navajo squash blossom necklace is the *naja,* an inverted crescent pendant that is a fertility symbol.

RAIN If you're getting married in a location where wet weather is likely (many gorgeous venues are significantly cheaper in the rainy off-season), embrace the idea of rain as a symbol of washing away the past, showering you with luck, fertility, and blessings from above, and strengthening your union because a wet knot is harder to untie. Adopt the umbrella, a common nuptial image, as your own. In Finland, through much of the twentieth century an escort held one over the bride's head as she went door to door collecting her dowry, making it a popular motif for Finnish weddings today (see page 52); in Tibet, Buddhists honor the White Umbrella Goddess as a sign of protection; in New Orleans, parasols make a joyous appearance during a second line parade (see page 120).

STARS Whether paired with a moon or on their own, these sparkling fireballs are a bright reminder of the stars in your eyes or a love story written in the stars. The North Star is a symbol of divine guidance that's lucky for sailors, and the starry sky has been said to represent all the children of Abraham.

SUN The sun and the direction it rises from are eloquent metaphors for a new beginning. This is why Navajo weddings take place facing east, the compass point associated with the future, so that the couple are looking toward their new life together.

TREES Another natural symbol that's universally understood as auspicious is the tree of life. It calls to mind a family tree, rooted in the past but spreading toward the future and up to the heavens. The Koran refers to the Tree of Immortality, and in the Bahá'í text *The Manifestation of God,* it is written "ye were all gathered in My presence beneath the shade of the tree of life, which is planted in the all-glorious paradise." Virtually every indigenous group in the Americas, from the Aztecs to the Zunis, holds trees sacred.

All over the world, different cultures find specific types of trees auspicious: Hindus favor a banyan while Buddhists believe that the Buddha was born under a pipal tree, making it lucky. Orthodox Christians view cypress trees as representations of souls ascending to heaven and plant them to mark sacred sites. Norse mythology refers to the Yggdrasil, or "world tree," which may be a yew, an ash, or the oak tree sacred to the god Thor. And fruiting trees are a global hallmark of fertility.

Dutch marriage traditions include the wedding wish tree: in the Netherlands, a potted tree is displayed at the reception and guests are given leaf-shaped tags on which to write messages to the newlyweds; then they attach their good wishes to the branches with ribbons. Dutch couples also sit under a canopy made of evergreens prior to the wedding as a sign of everlasting love.

THE SHAPE OF THINGS TO COME

Man-made symbols have also been imbued with meaning throughout the ages and across cultures. One of the shapes below would add style and substance to your décor.

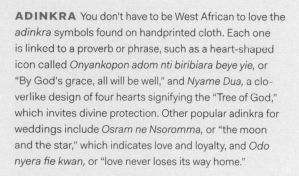

ADINKRA You don't have to be West African to love the *adinkra* symbols found on handprinted cloth. Each one is linked to a proverb or phrase, such as a heart-shaped icon called *Onyankopon adom nti biribiara beye yie,* or "By God's grace, all will be well," and *Nyame Dua,* a cloverlike design of four hearts signifying the "Tree of God," which invites divine protection. Other popular adinkra for weddings include *Osram ne Nsoromma,* or "the moon and the star," which indicates love and loyalty, and *Odo nyera fie kwan,* or "love never loses its way home."

BRAIDS This profound design—which can appear anywhere from silk cords to decorative bread—is made of two intertwined strands (or, in some cases, three, which is perfect if one of you has a child). Braided hair has significance of its own (see pages 70–71).

DOUBLE HAPPINESS In China, wedding guests don't sign a guest book but instead write their names on a cloth bearing a Double Happiness symbol, which the couple can hang in their home after the ceremony. According to legend, the motif, which shows the character for *happy,* repeated and linked, was developed by two young lovers.

HEARTS Inspired by the actual shape of the human organ, the heart is understood everywhere as a herald of love, perhaps because the ancient Greeks imagined the soul lived within the heart. It is, after all, what flutters when you feel a strong emotion.

HORSESHOES English brides may walk down the aisle carrying decorative horseshoes, which have been considered lucky since the ancient Celts believed iron could scare away goblins. Horseshoes engraved with the couple's names are now a common gift the bride can carry on the day and display at home after the event. A variant of this tradition in the American South has a small child handing the bride a decorated horseshoe as she walks back up the aisle.

INFINITY Resembling the lucky number 8 on its side (see pages 32–33), this symbol is elegant and meaningful, as it has no beginning and no end.

KNOTS There's a reason you're said to be tying one on your wedding day—it binds two different strands together. Hindus and Buddhists especially prize the mystical knot, which has eight loops, represents endless love, and happens to resemble the Celtic love knot.

MONOGRAMS A crest incorporating your initials is an elegant touch. But if you're changing your name, don't use your new, shared last initial until after the ceremony, when it actually *is* your initial, sacramentally speaking. To slap that letter onto invitations or programs would invite bad juju. Using it as a cake topper at the reception, though, would be fine. What if you happen to have the same last initial? An English proverb dating back to the mid-1800s states "to change the name but not the letter is to change for the worse and not the better." Ignore it. It's a good omen according to your own, personal folklore.

WHEEL OF LIFE A potent icon in Buddhism, this circle has no beginning and no end.

BAD LUCK BUSTERS

They say an ounce of prevention is worth a pound of cure. And when it comes to bad luck, believe it. Luckily, you've got history on your side to fight any negativity that may be present at your wedding. Centuries of folk wisdom have developed universally agreed upon symbols that repel "the evil eye." In much of the Mediterranean, including Greece and Turkey, that's the color blue or an image of an eye itself—charms that are also referred to as "evil eyes." In Italy, Israel, and other countries, the color red fights the evil eye. Cornuti, red charms shaped like the Devil's horn, or like a hand making a horn shape with the pointer and pinkie fingers, are popular amulets in southern Italy. Mirrors deflect the evil eye back at its giver—and anything that reflects light, like sequins, counts, too.

Another lovely misfortune-stopper is an image of an open, five-fingered palm, known as the *hamsa*, the Arabic word for *five*. Popular in the Middle East, it is also called the Hand of Miriam, for Moses's sister, the Hand of Mary, and the Hand of Fatima, after the daughter of the Prophet Mohammed. It tells bad luck to "talk to the hand," and has been doing so since ancient Mesopotamia, where the symbol of divine protection was associated with the goddess Ishtar. (Hands in general make an apt wedding motif, as the bride is seen as giving her hand in marriage.) And, don't forget, tassels also have the power to swish away the evil eye.

CHAPTER SEVEN

LOVE
IN BLOOM

The Secrets of Wedding Flowers

T hey're symbols of love, vitality, and fertility, so it's hardly a surprise that flowers have been an integral part of weddings since ancient times, when Greek brides wore floral crowns and Roman ones carried garlands with strong-smelling herbs to ward off evil spirits. In the medieval era, an aisle strewn with aromatic flower petals also made the church smell better, given that people didn't bathe as often. Today, flowers add to the luck and fragrance of a wedding, and to its sacred nature. Beautiful blooms are a sign that something momentous is happening right now. And because flowers have such an established association with symbolic meanings, one of the prettiest parts of your day can also be one of the luckiest.

FLOWER POWER

Back in Victorian times, when social media was nonexistent and social mores were more restrained, it could be hard to tell how others were feeling. Many courting couples relied on the language of flowers, exchanging blossoms that had universally understood significance. Some of the most romantic associations are listed below. If you love the flower and the meaning, work it into your bouquet or centerpieces. Or pass out the petals of meaningful blooms for attendees to toss as you walk back up the aisle.

Camellias
Equal admiration

Baby's breath
Everlasting love

Carnations
Pure love

Holly
Happiness in a home

Daisies
Love and innocence

Ivy
Marital love, friendship, and loyalty

Lilacs
First love

Lilies
Purity (if they're white),
beauty (calla lilies),
wealth (tiger lilies),
and a return to happiness
(lilies of the valley)

Myrtle
Love

Orange blossoms
Eternal love and fertility

Peonies
Marital love

Orchids
Fecundity and beauty

Roses
Love

Stephanotis
Marital happiness

Snowdrops
Hope

Tulips
Love

Zinnias
Long-term love or
longing for absent friends

Violets
Modesty and loyalty

The Victorians aren't the only ones who ascribed significance to certain flowers. Ancient Greeks considered myrtle to be the flower of Aphrodite, goddess of love, and often incorporated it into wedding ceremonies. Back in Tudor days, English brides carried marigolds, which were thought to be an aphrodisiac—and sometimes ate the edible flowers after the ceremony. (They do look amazing in salads, drinks, and desserts, should you want to get your guests in the mood.) Chinese, Indian, Persian, and many European cultures believe orange blossoms signify purity, innocence, and fertility, because they come from a tree that produces both a fruit and a flower. British brides often carry lily of the valley (as Kate Middleton did). The flower is linked to purity and a return to happiness and is associated with Ostara (or Eostre), the Germanic goddess of spring and fertility, and with the Virgin Mary, as it is said to have sprung from the tears she cried at the Crucifixion. Irish brides may include lavender in their bouquet to symbolize devotion. In the Alps, edelweiss is a popular sign of love and bravery because it can be so treacherous to climb the mountains where it grows. In China, where peonies and chrysanthemums bring luck and prosperity, they are embroidered on the bride's dress and incorporated into wedding flowers. And in Korea, peonies symbolize marital happiness, love, and passion, and are worked into the wedding table display (see page 91). Polynesians consider ti leaves from the evergreen *cordyline fruticosa* lily sacred; the officiant blesses the bride and groom with the leaves to drive off evil spirits and invite kind ones, then ties their wrists together with a garland made of them.

It's always lucky to incorporate your culture and personality into your wedding. If your background can be represented by a flower—whether it's bells of Ireland or camellias (the state flower of Alabama)—add it to your bouquet. Select flowers that are significant for your personal history: the blossoms your mother carried in her bouquet, the variety you always have in your apartment, or the blooms one of you sent the other after your first date. Or follow the Italian custom of having your groom choose the bouquet. Traditionally, in Italy, the groom would pick the flowers the morning of the wedding and offer them to the bride as a final courting present. Nowadays he's more likely to simply pay for the bouquet. If you like the romance of the groom giving the bride the bouquet, but aren't about to have him stand outside the church holding it as he awaits your arrival, as is done in Greece, consider having him bring it to the "first look," if you're taking photos before the wedding (see page 58).

That's a Wrap

Bouquets are beautiful, and they also give you something to do with your nervous hands as you walk down the aisle. How a clutch is held together can be as meaningful as the blooms themselves. Wrapping stems with a knotted ribbon draws on the tradition of the Hercules knot at the waist of Roman brides' gowns, which could be undone only by their husbands. Bouquets can also have hanging ribbons with the ends tied into "lovers' knots"; according to a British custom, each one was a wish for the couple's future (see page 88). The knots were auspicious for one lucky bridesmaid, too—whoever caught the bouquet (see page 47) got to untie one while making a wish she was assured would come true.

You could secure your bouquet with an heirloom handkerchief, or the "magic hankie" you plan to turn into your child's christening bonnet, according to Irish tradition (see pages 75–76). Or you might pin a brooch with a photo of an absent relative or friend onto the fabric that wraps the stems. You could even skip tying the stems altogether and incorporate loved ones into the making of the bouquet by having guests line the aisle holding flowers that you gather into your hands as you walk toward your spouse-to-be, collecting their blessings along with the blooms.

This Bud's for You

The bride is not the only person accessorizing with flowers; bridesmaids tote bouquets, too. When designing bridesmaids' bouquets, you may want to add ivy, which signifies friendship. Also appropriate are ranunculus, which symbolize radiance and charm; jasmine for amiability; and white roses, which indicate worth, a subtle sign of how much you value your friends. Or share some of the luck from the bridal bouquet by giving each bridesmaid a posy made up of one single variety of a flower included in your own clutch. Another idea is to have bridesmaids or flower girls carry mini varieties of the flower you're bringing down the aisle—think tea roses if you're holding roses. A Welsh tradition that mixes sharing luck with divination has the bride carry a bouquet of myrtle and give a live sprig of it to her bridesmaids. They're all supposed to plant their cuttings after the wedding; it's said that if it takes root and grows, that bridesmaid will marry within a year.

Herbs and berries make handsome boutonnieres, and some have folkloric significance—rosemary symbolizes remembrance; sage indicates wisdom; basil is for everlasting love; parsley, joy; dill, cheerfulness; coriander, hidden worth; cumin, fidelity; marjoram, happiness; oregano, substance; thyme, courage; and chives, good luck. Or pick a symbolic stem that's a nod to your background; Scottish grooms deem it lucky to wear a sprig of white heather and a Scottish thistle as a boutonniere. You could extend that idea to other countries by turning their national flowers into bouts: a red poppy for Belgium, Cattelya orchid for Brazil, maple leaf for Canada, calla lily for Ethiopia, tulip for Holland, shamrock for Ireland, king protea for South Africa, or coffee flower for Yemen. Or consider giving each groomsmen a single stem of his home state's flower.

Gracious Garlands

Having bridesmaids wear floral crowns has become such a trend that some brides-to-be host a wreath-making party, where attendants craft their own headpieces. More classic brides might limit floral crowns to the flower girl. But whoever wears a wreath in her hair is following an ancient tradition. The Greeks and Romans used wreaths made of laurel leaves or olive branches to crown winners of the Olympic games, politicians at festivities, and brides. Later, the Romans expanded wreaths to include flowers, especially at Floralia, the festival of the nature goddess (see page 27), who was often shown holding a floral crown. And under her long veil a Roman bride would wear her hair braided with ribbons and topped with a wreath of sacred herbs and flowers.

Fast-forward to trendy Queen Victoria, who wore a wreath of orange blossoms at her wedding in 1840, sparking a trend that shows no sign of stopping—and *she* could have worn a real crown if she'd wanted! A traditional Hungarian headdress, decorated in flowers, contained sheaves of wheat as a sign of fecundity, while Czech brides wore a rosemary wreath made by the bridesmaids for the same reason. And Hawaiian brides still wear *haku* leis, a sort of floral halo, around their forehead (and sometimes around their wrists or ankles, too).

In Switzerland, the bride's floral crown was burned after the wedding; the faster it was consumed by fire, the luckier she was said to be.

Sacred Stems

In some cultures, blossoms, plants, or trees are part of the ritual itself. In Orthodox Christian weddings in Greece, guests throw rose petals and rice over the couple as they circle the altar for the third time in the Dance of Isaiah (see page 114), the exact moment when they're considered married. The petals and rice are to shower the pair with good luck and fertility. The first ritual of the four-day Zoroastrian wedding is the *mândav-saro,* in which a mango tree is planted by the door of the couple's home to invite fertility. A milestone in a Hindu wedding is the swapping of floral garlands as *The Ramayana* describes the goddess Sita placing one around Lord Ram's neck to show she wishes him to be her husband. Mortal women follow suit at the start of the ceremony, ringing the *varmala,* or groom's garland, around their intended's neck before he places the *jaimala* around hers.

Leis, which symbolize joy and eternal love, play a substantial role in certain island cultures. Hawaiian and Polynesian couples exchange them during their ceremonies, and may give leis to their parents to thank them. In Hawaii, the groom will usually receive an open-ended lei of maile vines, draped around his neck like an opera scarf, while brides often choose the pikake flower, a type of white jasmine. The officiant, or *kahuna pule,* will wrap a lei around the couple's joined hands. Tahitian bride's lei go-tos are the local gardenia known as *tiare* and hibiscus. If you're joining families, exchanging leis with your children can be a powerful ritual, as leis, like rings, are round, and therefore symbols of everlasting love.

Sometimes flowers aren't in the ceremony, but above it. A Jewish wedding takes place beneath a chuppah, which represents the home the newlyweds will build together. The word means "covered with garlands," but any canopy, such as a cloth held by four posts, can do the job. Hindu ceremonies take place under a tent-like structure, called a *mandap,* which is held by four pillars to represent the parents who raised the couple. It is often decorated with garlands of flowers and mango leaves to create a fragrant, stunning setting.

The end of the ceremony doesn't mean the end of lucky floral rituals. Flower petals are among the many things that may be tossed at couples as they leave the church or their reception, to show joy and send the pair luck. (Many cultures go for roses, but in Spain, the Roma prefer almond blossoms, which are symbols of fertility.) In Indonesia, the flowers show up at the reception—the bride and groom walk into the party passing by the *pagar ayu,* or "fence of beauty," formed by family members holding a chain of blooms to welcome the newlyweds.

Do Me a Favor

Flora make great favors, whether it's potted herbs with a tag describing their significance, a mini plant, a terrarium, an evergreen sapling (like your evergreen love), or cut flowers. Traditionally, Czech bridesmaids would pin a rosemary stem on each guest as he or she arrived, filling the wedding with the symbol of fertility. At Hindu weddings female guests often receive a small jasmine garland, a symbol of divine hope, to wrap around the bun in their hair, wrist, or whatever they see fit. A variation of either of these traditions would be to pin single blooms to escort cards or programs. At Polynesian and Hawaiian weddings, attendees receive floral leis upon arrival. In China and Taiwan, bamboo plants are often given as favors to guests and gifts to the couple, because they're strong but flexible, like a good relationship. Two stalks of bamboo braided together are especially lucky as a symbol of marriage, and three invite happiness. There's even historic precedent for flowers as favors: Elizabethan couples gave attendees corsages wrapped in ribbons, which they wore during the party and for the next few days, to invite luck and to extend the joy of the celebration.

THINK OUTSIDE THE (FLOWER) BOX

Flowers may grow on trees, but that doesn't mean they're inexpensive. Plenty of floral alternatives are more affordable and just as auspicious. Succulents make great centerpieces, look less feminine than many flowers (which can work well for double-groom ceremonies), and are considered lucky because they have incredible survival skills, like love itself. Herbs are meaningful, affordable, and traditional, too; Swedish brides and 'maids used stinky herbs and weeds in their bouquets to repel trolls. You might try more pleasant smelling lavender, rosemary, or eucalyptus instead. Small potted herbs lining the center of the table add up to an impressive long centerpiece that can be broken up at the end of the night by each guest bringing one home to plant, where it will grow along with your love.

Beyond herbs, there are grasses—clover is especially lucky if it's four-leafed (see page 84), and *durva* grass (also known as Bahama grass or Bermuda grass) is used in India as an offering to Ganesh. And don't overlook branches and leaves. Olive branches symbolize peace and fertility, and any fruiting branch represents, well, fruitfulness. Go old-school with a grain, like the sheaves of wheat Roman brides carried—or follow Indonesian custom by replacing centerpieces with *kembar mayang*, towering basket-like structures made of coconut leaves and covered in leaves folded into birds (which fly high), grasshoppers (which are energetic), and umbrellas (which are symbols of protection).

If your venue allows open flames, candles look romantic, cast a flattering light, symbolize love and hope, and cost less than flowers (see page 112). Pinecones, acorns, walnuts, hazelnuts, and chestnuts signify abundance, and show people you're nuts about each other (see page 136).

The Giving Trees

Walking under an allée or canopy of trees or branches is magical, beautiful, and some would say practical, too—florists swear that creating one big, memorable installation near the entrance of the reception is a way to save on flowers because it allows you to use fewer blooms elsewhere. Take inspiration from the Danish *aeresport*, "gate of honor," an arch of branches hung over the door of the bride's parents' house; the married couple create another one above their own door twenty-five years later, on their silver anniversary.

Decorating with potted trees is another option. In Japan, an orange tree provides the wow factor in terms of wedding décor. And in Thailand, banana trees represent fertility, and sugar cane adds even more sweetness to the day. Banana trees are also a common sight at weddings in Java because they're adaptable and can thrive in many varied environments, as the couple should.

And if you're getting married at home, a tree or perennial plant will continue to decorate your life long after the wedding itself. Traditionally, in old Czechoslovakia, the tree-planting took place the night before the wedding, when the bride's friends dug a hole in her yard, planted a young tree, roots and all, and hung decorated eggshells from it to surprise her when she woke up. In Holland and in Switzerland, the newlyweds plant a pine tree in the yard of their home themselves to invite luck and fertility. A Dutch pair might plant lily of the valley, which blooms every year, and is said to renew the couple's love for each other each time it does. In Bermuda, the newlyweds plant a cedar sapling (which might have been their cake topper, see page 144) to grow with their family. And a Victorian bride's attendants would plant myrtle at the newlyweds' home to invite happiness and supply the bridal bouquets of future generations.

CHAPTER EIGHT

MASTERING YOUR CEREMONY

Layer Luck into Your Wedding

Your ceremony is the moment all the other hoopla is celebrating, the instant you change your lives, pledging to live them together, forever. It's what everyone came to see. Wedding ceremonies vary among cultures, but all address a central theme: the joining together of two people. And most follow a certain order, incorporating some or all of the following: a processional to herald the arrival of the couple; a unity ritual to join two into one; a transition ritual to symbolize their embarking on a new journey together; a promise ritual that may include vows or a ring exchange; a legally binding contract; and a recessional, in which everybody leaves feeling a little more joyous. If you're marrying within an established religion or a cultural tradition you know well, the outline of your ceremony, and many of the rituals in it, have been established for you already. But that doesn't mean you can't introduce a few new, and auspicious, customs in the same way you might add spice to a beloved family recipe.

WALK THIS WAY

The idea of a bride or groom leaving a childhood home to get married is highly emotional, and rituals have developed to express those feelings. In the Balkans, the bride's family will dress her for the wedding, while singing ballads of loss, then switch to songs of joy, instructing the groom to treasure her, as they proceed to the ceremony. In England, Scotland, and many Slavic countries, there's the practice of warming the threshold, or pouring boiling water on the doorstep of the bride's house before she leaves for the wedding, to wash away her old life.

Another visible example of the bride leaving her natal family and joining her husband to create a new one is the processional inside the house of worship or ceremony space. Traditionally, in Christian faiths, she walks in with her father; in Jewish ceremonies, her parents escort her in together after the groom has walked in on the arms of his parents.

But in many cultures, the processional starts long before the ceremony as a prenuptial parade from the groom's home to the bride's to the venue. In Bulgaria, the groom's friends show up at his house, sprinkle him

with barley for luck and fertility, and shoot guns to scare off evil spirits. The groom asks his parents for their blessing, then they all proceed to the home of the best man, who has made a wedding banner out of scarves, ribbons, and fruit impaled on a branch from a fruit tree (see page 86). The best man leads everyone dancing to the bride's house, bringing her candles for light, wine for joy, sweets for a sweet life, and her veil. The bride, hiding in a locked room, lets in only the maid of honor. As the groom and best man bang on the door, the maid of honor tries to put the veil on the bride, who nixes it twice to indicate her reluctance to leave her childhood behind, then accepts it on the third try, to show she is ready for this new stage of life. Once she emerges, the couple are led outside where the bride throws a dish filled with wheat, a raw egg, and coins (signs of fertility and prosperity) into the air. It crashes—ostensibly in as many pieces as the pair will have children—and the group dances to the church where the they enter by stepping forward with their right legs, getting the marriage off on the right foot.

In Vietnam, the mother of the groom comes to the bride's house before the entire procession to let everyone know when the groom will arrive. She brings betel nuts to show respect for the bride's family and pink chalk to ensure a rosy future.

In France, where a civil ceremony is required, a pair may have a town hall wedding, then a religious ritual with the couple and their families making a processional from the government building to the house of worship on foot or in a cortege of cars.

A Hindu groom takes part in a procession, known as a *baraat*, in which he rides on a decorated horse or elephant, stopping to dance with his family and friends to the music of the live band accompanying them, until they reach the bride's family. There, her relatives will make him submit to a few tests of his intelligence and dexterity before exchanging floral garlands as a sign of the families' acceptance of each other.

In several cultures, when the parade reaches the bride's house, ritual games take place to symbolize her relatives' reluctance to part with her. In Armenian families, for example, a child will steal one of the bride's wedding shoes so she can't leave, until the maid of honor pays the kid to get the shoe back, and a brother or uncle will stand at the door with a weapon until the groom and best man bribe him to step aside. In the last century, in parts of Wales, when the bride reached the church her relatives would "abduct" her, and the groom's side would follow in hot pursuit. Whoever caught her was said to be next to marry, but the ritual, called "marriage by capture," recalls the Middle Ages when grooms would kidnap their brides.

Historically, a woman in transition to becoming a wife was considered at risk of falling prey to bad luck en route to her wedding. A Chinese bride in days past would be carried to the ceremony in a red sedan chair, with a red veil over her face and gongs sounding or fireworks exploding to scare off evil spirits. In Britain, many superstitions arose surrounding what constituted a good or bad omen for the bride to spot on the way to the ceremony, some of which are still repeated today: doves, lambs, and—just on this occasion—black cats are auspicious. Cats are often considered magical beasts, and in medieval times, it was said to be good luck for the family cat to sneeze at the bride or groom the morning of the wedding. But the luckiest sight of all is a chimney sweep. Since they're hard to find these days, a British bride may hire one to stop by on the morning of the wedding to give her a good-luck kiss and to shake the groom's hand (as Prince Phillip did before marrying Queen Elizabeth in 1947).

Bridal processions from home to home were easier when everyone lived near one another in small villages. But if your future in-laws are local, or you're having a destination wedding at a camp or resort, it might be fun to parade around, inviting good luck all along the way.

COME TOGETHER

An entire wedding could be considered a unity ritual, but some cultures and couples choose to drive the point home with a visual representation of two people linking their lives together. Unlike many customs that are gender-based or focus on fertility, these unity rituals work well for any engaged pair.

One option is the lighting of a unity candle. Each member of the couple holds a lit candle, which they bring together at the same time to light a single taper. When both flames meet, the light created is brighter than each individual candle was alone. The two original flames may be left burning, to symbolize the fact that the newlyweds' individual souls will continue to thrive, and their parents may light candles to indicate both families are coming together. Although the unity candle is a relatively recent Christian tradition that surged in popularity in the 1980s after Luke and Laura lit one on the soap opera *General Hospital,* candlelight represents hope and warmth in virtually every culture, as well as the light of God in several religions, making it a highly auspicious symbol (see page 84).

A less flammable unity ritual is tree planting (see page 103), in which the members of the couple each take earth from different containers, perhaps brought from their home countries or childhood backyards, and use the soil to cover the roots of a sapling (usually one that has been largely planted prior to the wedding) at the site of the ceremony. This act signals the start of the family tree the couple will nurture together.

Another mixing of two elements into one is the sand ceremony, believed to have originated in Hawaii. Each member of the pair holds a clear vase, cup, or tube of sand from a beach that has significance to him or her, or in a color distinguishable from their partner's. Taking turns, each pours the sand into a third vessel, where the grains mix together so that it's impossible for them to ever be separated.

Handfasting is one unity ritual common to many cultures (see page 18). The Celtic version dates back to sixteenth-century Scotland and involves the couple joining hands and the officiant tying them together with ribbon. Ukrainians cover the joined hands with a wedding *rushnyk,* a ceremonial cloth embroidered in red, auspicious designs, such as a duck and a drake, which symbolize the bride and groom.

A couple may also be bound together in the Hispanic *lazo* ritual, in which a friend or relative loops a silk ribbon, rope, or two linked five-decade rosaries around the pair in a figure-eight infinity symbol so they'll be joined for all eternity (see page 44). Chinese pairs may choose to be tied to each other with a strand of red silk, to recall the invisible cord that connected them since birth until fate brought them together.

In a custom called *mala badol,* South Asian Muslims drape a cloth over the couple as they feed each other ritual food and drink. Then there's the Polynesian tradition of wrapping the pair in a *tei fa fa,* a special quilt sewn for the wedding that will later decorate their home. Eastern Cherokee couples were traditionally bound together by a blanket during their ceremonies. And another Ukrainian custom involves a special embroidered rug called a *pidnozhnyk,* or "step-on towel," that the couple stands on at the wedding. It creates a space the pair occupies together and is meant to ensure they never stand on a bare floor, that is, know poverty.

Sometimes, a simple act of sharing represents the couple's union. In Jewish and Orthodox Christian ceremonies, the bride and groom drink from the same glass of wine, a common "cup of experience" that represents all they will share in the future. Buddhist couples sip sake from three special *sakazuki* cups in a ritual known as the *san-san-kudo,* or "three, three, nine," because each person drinks from each one thrice. And in France, the newlyweds sip from an elaborate *coupe de marriage,* which is often engraved silver. If you don't drink alcohol, consider sharing a symbolic food (see page 134); Persian couples dip a finger in honey to feed each other at the end of their ceremonies.

Some pairs involve their guests in the unity ritual, inviting their blessings. A wedding-wide show of unity can be as simple as holding your ceremony in the round, with attendees seated in a circle around you, as in a Quaker friendship circle. Or the officiant may ask the assembled group, "Who will support this couple throughout their marriage?" seeking the answer "We will." Otherwise, the attendees can partake in an adaptation of a couple's unity ritual. If you like the image of candlelight, consider having a display of unlit votive candles at the entrance of your ceremony space with a sign inviting guests to light one and help brighten your future. Or follow the Moravian Czech tradition of passing the unity flame lit by the bride and groom from guest to guest, with each one holding an unlit candle until the light of love reaches them. At Thai weddings, an elder ties a *sai sin,* a sacred thread blessed by Buddhist monks, around each of the newlyweds' wrists, and in central Thailand, guests follow suit, also tying holy threads around the bride's and groom's arms.

Even the ring exchange can become a communal rite if you follow another new wedding custom that gained currency in secular American weddings: a ring-warming or blessing of the rings, in which the wedding bands (secured to an object, such as a ribbon or pillow) are passed around so that friends and family can imbue them with their wishes for the couple, whether silently, or speaking their blessings aloud.

EMBRACE CHANGE

Joining two people together is one aspect of a marriage; the couple adopting a new way of life is another, one that is often marked by a transition ritual. Many cultures, including the Roma in Europe, have some version of jumping the broom, as the cleaning tool is a strong symbol of a home, and jumping over it shows a willingness to enter into a new household. Also a custom in some West African wedding ceremonies, jumping the broom became popular in the United States before the Civil War when slaves, who were prohibited from marrying legally, would hold their own ceremonies, placing a broom on the floor, then leaping over it holding hands. In some variations, the groom sets the broom facing north before the couple jump, then the bride turns it to face the south and they hop over it again. The ritual is meant to sweep away bad luck, and to let everyone assembled know that this pair is bounding into a new life together.

Other communities have the couple take a short journey together to represent the fact that they're setting off on a new, joint venture. In the Dance of Isaiah, Orthodox Christian couples walk around an altar table three times, holding hands and linked by a ribbon that ties together their *stefana* crowns (see page 69). On the third circle, they're officially married. In the Hindu ceremony, the couple embark on the *saptapadi,* seven sacred steps around a fire. Each step represents a blessing and wish for their future (see page 116). In a traditional Jewish wedding, the bride circles the groom seven times, which reflects the process of God creating the world in seven days—and the new world the couple will create together.

While many of these transition rituals emphasize walking toward the future, others focus on releasing the past. This letting go can be symbolized by a water ritual, in which holy water is poured, often from a shell, over the hands of the couple to purify them of any past negativity. The bride and groom wash each other's hands in Navajo ceremonies, while in Polynesia, the officiant pours the water over the newlyweds' hands, and in a Thai water blessing, the couple's parents do the honors. Many African communities use water in their ceremonies as well, but its purpose is more an offering to God and departed ancestors, asking for their blessings. This libation ritual may be performed with alcohol instead, with the officiant or a family elder pouring the spirit onto the ground in four directions and praying for love, health, and abundance.

One powerful symbolic act that marks a break with the past is the groom stomping on a glass at the end of a Jewish wedding. Theologically, it's a reminder of the destruction of the Temple in Jerusalem—that even in times of great joy, there is sorrow in the world. Folk interpretations include the idea that smashing the glass to bits means the marriage will endure until the goblet is put back together again (i.e., forever). Others say that the number of pieces it breaks into foretells the number of children the pair will have or the number of years they'll live together. In Java, as part of the ceremony, the groom steps on a raw egg, cracking it to demonstrate his willingness to become a father before the bride washes his feet to show she will always take care of him.

TAKE A VOW

Vows may be spoken by the newlyweds-to-be, as in Western ceremonies that end with each member of the couple promising "I do," but we'll get to that on page 124. Alternatively, they may be recited by the officiant or loved ones, as is the case with the Sheva B'rachot, the seven blessings in a Jewish wedding. These thank God for creating "the fruit of the vine" (wine), which represents joy; "all things to Your glory," which is to say the universe; "humankind"; and "man in Your image after Your Likeness, and woman from man as his companion." They then ask that the bride and groom have children, become loving companions, and experience everlasting joy. Traditionally, the final blessing praises God and reminds us that joy is greater when it is shared: "Blessed are You, Adonai, who rejoices with the bride and groom," but some couples tailor the blessings to their circumstance, perhaps adding an eighth to reflect a same-sex pair's experience (often referencing Jonathan and King David). If you don't identify with the Jewish religion, you might still borrow the idea of having loved ones recite words of thanks and wishes for the future. Choose blessings from your culture or religion, write your own expressions of thanks and hope, or read from family documents, such as grandpa's love letters to grandma.

Sometimes the blessings are improvisational. During a Quaker wedding, everyone sits in silence until someone feels moved to get up and relate a sentiment to, or wish for, the couple. This approach works best for a small wedding, and if you've included a note in your invitation giving guests a heads up.

Other vows are unspoken, but represented in movement, such as the *saptapadi,* or seven steps around the sacred fire, in a Hindu ceremony. Each step represents a hope or wish for the future. The first is for the couple to provide nourishment for their household; the second, that they grow stronger physically, mentally, and spiritually; and the third, that they prosper. The fourth is a petition to grow in joy, love, and trust; the fifth, that they have children; the sixth, that they enjoy a long life together; and the seventh, that they remain lifelong friends and partners. Even if you're not taking symbolic actions you might think about what you wish for your marriage and share those aspirations in your vows.

Whatever words are (or aren't) said, many cultures also include an exchange of rings as a physical representation of the newlyweds' vow to love each other until death do they part (see page 14). Think of the sixteenth-century vow that says, "This ring is round and hath no end / So is my love unto my friend." The vast majority of couples exchange rings as symbols of their love, some (Catholics, Protestants, many nondenominational couples) while reciting vows, others (Orthodox Christians, Orthodox Jews) remaining silent and letting the physical exchange speak for itself. According to Jewish tradition, the rings used in the ceremony should be solid gold bands to represent the whole, unbroken promise the couple are making to each other. For this reason, many couples exchange heirloom bands, with the bride opting for great-great-grandma's solid gold ring in the ceremony (as opposed to the gem-studded eternity band she may wear day-to-day). Partners bringing children into a marriage can follow a new tradition by exchanging meaningful jewelry with them as well, whether that's rings for the kids or a "family medallion," a pendant of three circles created by Roger Coleman, a minister in Kansas City in 1987, which has since become an emblem of blended marriage.

While you're exchanging bands, think about where to place them. The third finger of the left hand is considered lucky in the United States and many other countries—some say so because it's the only one that can't extend itself to its full potential without another finger by its side. The same finger is also customary in Western Europe, where it was once romantically, but mistakenly, thought that a vein from there led directly to the heart. But Balkan and other cultures choose the third finger of the right hand, perhaps because of the Bible description of Jesus sitting to the right hand of the Father. (For more on ring placement, see page 14.)

Rings aren't the only precious items that represent the promises the couple are making to each other. In Hispanic weddings, after the priest blesses the thirteen coins known as the *arras* (see pages 44–45), the couple pass them back and forth, symbolizing a vow to love each other for richer and for poorer. The number 13 may represent Jesus and the Apostles. But in some ceremonies, each of the coins is assigned a specific marital virtue: love, trust, commitment, respect, joy, happiness, harmony, wisdom, nurturing, caring, cooperation, wholeness, and peace.

KEEP IT LEGAL

The rituals of a wedding are meaningful, but it wouldn't be a legitimate ceremony without a legal document to make things official. At a Jewish wedding, the signing of the ketubah kicks off the festivities (see page 58). While these contracts state the terms of the marriage, they are also often beautiful works of art the couple can display in their home to recall the promises they made. Muslim weddings vary between geographic and cultural groups, but wherever the ceremony is held, what actually makes the event a wedding is the signing of the *nikkah,* or "marriage covenant." In the case of both the ketubah and the nikkah, the signature of witnesses is required to make the marriage official, a reminder that we're all part of a community.

Similarly, Quaker couples have everyone present sign a certificate that states the attendees witnessed the wedding and will support the newlyweds in their life together. Because Quakers don't have clergypeople, believing that only God can join a couple together, it's as if the guests officiated the marriage. You might have a calligrapher draw up a document of support modeled on a Quaker wedding certificate and ask attendees to sign it instead of a guest book.

SEE YOU AT THE RECEPTION

Many ceremonies end with a moment of levity, or at least noise, to break the solemnity and tension. That might be the newlyweds kissing for the first time as a married couple and everyone cheering, the breaking of the glass (see page 115), or the ringing of bells to scare off evil spirits and express joy, as in the Irish and Scottish countryside. The last steps of a Muslim ceremony may include the salaam, in which the groom blesses the guests, and the *savaqu,* where the attendees toss coins at the bride. Romanians also throw coins at the bride's feet as she walks back up the aisle so that the couple may enjoy prosperity and abundance in their married life. At the end of Sikh weddings in a ritual called *doli,* the bride's female relatives dress her in new clothing and jewelry and she throws rice behind herself, bidding farewell to her old life, before the couple depart.

Speaking of throwing things, the toss that happens when the pair leaves the ceremony is a chance for the guests, and the couple being showered with their well-wishes, to celebrate the fact that the pair is now officially Mr. and Mrs. (or Mr. and Mr. or Mrs. and Mrs.). It's one of the luckiest moments at a wedding, too, as, along with the physical objects being thrown, the newlyweds are covered in blessings. You might have your attendants pass out petals of symbolic flowers or herbs for throwing. Or, if you want children, stick with the classic fertility symbols of seeds and grains, which have been a hit since the ancient Greeks and Romans lobbed them at newlyweds. Rice is most popular in the United States, where it's said that if a bride has some stuck in her hair at the end of the night, she'll have a child within a year, and in Finland, where the number of grains she plucks from her hair foretells how many children she'll have. In France, wedding guests throw wheat, in Italy, it's candy and Jordan almonds for a sweet life, and in the Czech Republic, Moravians throw peas. In Sicily, guests mix up the grains, throwing barley to call forth baby boys and wheat for little girls. In Morocco, the toss takes place as the newlyweds leave the reception, not the ceremony, and guests shower the couple with figs and raisins instead of rice.

Whether loved ones offer their well-wishes at the end of the ceremony or the start of a reception, in Western cultures it's considered good luck to kiss the bride before the groom, so she stands first in the receiving line. And in New Orleans, the newlyweds may lead guests from the ceremony to the reception (or the party to their next stop) in a parade called a second line, carrying parasols while the guests wave handkerchiefs at them as a band plays. The name comes from the "second line" of revelers following the band in a parade. Other traditional processions couples adopt as their walk from ceremony to reception include the Bahamian *junkanoo,* with dressed-up musicians and dancers leading the march, and the *callejoneada,* from Guanajuato, Mexico, a walking serenade led by a band and costumed revelers.

CHAPTER NINE

USE YOUR WORDS

The Phrases That Make All the Difference

Whether or not you actually utter those two little syllables— "I do"—words of commitment, love, gratitude, joy, and hope will fill your wedding. They will be printed on marriage contracts or programs, spoken during your ceremony, and whispered to you on the dance floor. Some of the most meaningful will be private interactions with your new spouse or cherished guests. Others will be proclaimed publicly, for all to hear, giving your wedding its own personality. When it comes to the words you choose—as your vows, the readings in your ceremony, the lyrics to your first dance song, a toast you make, or even a wedding hashtag that helps guests share photos on social media—it's easy to make sure they're auspicious. And unlike clothing, flowers, or cake, words, while priceless, don't cost a thing, which is pretty darn lucky . . .

VOWS THAT WOW

Marriage vows may be the greatest proof that magic words exist. As soon as they're uttered, not one, but two, people are transformed. To reflect this fact, Polynesian wedding ceremonies end with the priest giving the couple a shared "marriage" name to reflect their new identities as spouses—a popular choice is Herenui, which means "big love." Whether your vows are traditional or original, spoken by you or by an officiant, or even enacted physically as you walk around the sacred fire in a Hindu ceremony (see page 116), or the altar in an Orthodox Christian one (see page 114), the promise you are making is life changing.

If you're having a traditional ceremony within an organized religion, then your vows are likely already provided for you. If you're writing your own vows, you may still want to draw on blessings from the marriage rite of an established religious tradition, whether it's your own, your spouse's, or a culture whose words speak to you. (See page 115 for more on rituals and blessings.)

Many traditional Western ceremonies have the couple recite simple standard vows, but leave room for creativity by letting them pick ceremony readings. For Catholic weddings, some readings need to be from the Bible. For non-biblical readings, you have options ranging from ancient texts to modern pop songs. If you're not sure where to start, go to the couples whose marriages you admire most, and ask what was read at their wedding. That's definitely something old—*and* something borrowed (see page 77)!

You could also look to poetry or prose by your favorite author or a writer from your cultural tradition, whether you quote her work or his love letters. (Who can forget F. Scott Fitzgerald's note to Zelda, "You are the finest, loveliest, tenderest, and most beautiful person I have ever known and even that is an understatement"?) Or select a text that is significant to you, even if it's not "romantic" per se; many couples quote the ruling on Goodridge v. Department of Public Health, in which the Chief Justice of the Massachusetts Supreme Court made same-sex marriage legal in the state, arguing that "the decision whether and whom to marry is among life's momentous acts of self-definition." Whatever vows you choose, if they're particularly meaningful to you, you may want to have them printed for guests to follow along or to save as a keepsake.

YOU SAID YOU WANTED A LOVE SONG?

Written and spoken words will add meaning to your day, but music will provide a soundtrack to everything from your ceremony to your last dance. Again, look to your cultural history and your own personal history to bring eloquence to your choices—if you and your dad danced to a favorite song when you were little, make that your father-daughter number. Here are some songs that scream—no, sing—good luck.

"ALLELUIA" Mozart's composition from Exsultate Jubilate is ideal for a religious ceremony or to add profound emotion to a secular one.

"AMAZING GRACE" The old spiritual makes a beautiful processional or musical selection for the ceremony, and nods to how amazing love of all kinds is.

"AT LAST" Etta James's bluesy ballad is a go-to for a reason; it celebrates the arrival of true love, or a happy ending that comes better late than never.

"GOD ONLY KNOWS" The Beach Boys' song is a (catchy) meditation on luck and love.

"THE LUCKIEST" This tune by Ben Folds sings the praises of joining up with your one and only.

"LUCKY" Jason Mraz croons about what it's like to fall in love with your best friend. Spoiler alert: the title pretty much sums it up.

"MAYBE I'M AMAZED" Paul McCartney's song, which describes the feeling of disbelief at having found a soul mate, is a touching first dance choice to express how lucky you feel.

"ODE TO JOY" The title of Beethoven's soaring composition says it all.

"YOU'RE JUST TOO GOOD TO BE TRUE" Whether you go for the Frankie Valli original or the sultry Fugees remake, this number is an ode to long-awaited love.

"WHAT A WONDERFUL WORLD" Being grateful is half of being lucky, making this homage to the globe and all the people in it a spot-on choice for a first dance or parent-child number.

TOASTS WITH THE MOST

Toasts have been an expression of affection since ancient Greece—*The Iliad* includes a scene in which Odysseus drinks to Achilles's health—and the reason we toast with our right hands held out in front of us may come from the Greeks raising wineglasses to the sky to praise the gods. Another theory holds the custom dates to the belligerent Middle Ages, when a raised arm showed that the person toasting had come in friendship and didn't have weapons concealed in his clothing. One exception to the no-weapons rule laces a champagne toast with luck: *sabrage,* the act of opening a bottle of bubbly with a ceremonial saber, is said to have started in Napoleon's army, when the soldiers wanted to celebrate a good outcome in battle, but remains popular at weddings—especially military ones—today. Even if there's swordplay involved, the spoken words are the most memorable aspect of any toast.

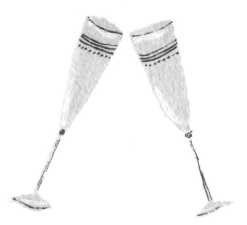

Raising a toast can be intimidating, but many cultures already have beautiful phrases for wishing newlyweds—or their loved ones—all the luck in the world. Some come from sacred texts, others are part of an oral tradition. When choosing texts, find something that makes you think, "Yes, that's exactly what I feel," then worry about its provenance. A commonly quoted "Apache Wedding Blessing"—"Now you will feel no rain, for each of you will be shelter to one another"—actually originated with the 1947 novel *Blood Brother* and became famous in the 1950 movie *Broken Arrow.* That shouldn't keep you from including it in your wedding ceremony if it resonates—inspiration can come from any number of places—although you'll probably want to cite its source accurately. Following are some culturally specific toasts and texts you can impart to guests, print on favor tags, or share with a nervous best man eager to toast you both.

From a Speaker to the Couple

Most of the toasting pressure will fall on other people—traditionally, that's your parents, if they're acting as hosts of the evening, the best man, and maid of honor. If an attendant asks you, "What should I say?" tell him or her to abstain from politics and exes, and offer these traditional expressions of congratulations as inspiration.

AFRICAN "May your love be like the misty rain, gentle coming in but flooding the river."

ARMENIAN "May you grow old on one pillow." Or "May your joys be as bright as the morning and your sorrows but shadows that fade into the sunlight of love."

BIBLICAL "May you live to see your children's children" (Psalm 128).

ENGLISH "May your joy be as sweet as the spring flowers that grow, as bright as a fire when winter winds blow, as countless as leaves that float down in the fall, as serene as the love that keeps watch over us all."

GREEK "The heart that loves is always young." Or consider Plato's "Love is the joy of the good, the wonder of the wise, the amazement of the Gods."

HAWAIIAN "May you never thirst again."

HINDU This passage from the *Brahma Sutra* celebrates the contagious nature of the couple's happiness: "When the one man loves the one woman, and the one woman loves the one man, the very angels desert heaven and sit in that hour and sing for joy."

IRISH "May the road rise to meet you. May the wind be always at your back, the sunshine warm upon your face, the rain fall soft upon your fields, and until we meet again, may God hold you in the hollow of His hand. May God be with you and bless you. May you see your children's children. May you be poor in misfortune, rich in blessings. May you know nothing but happiness from this day forward. May pure be the joys that surround you. May true be the hearts that love you."

JEWISH This marriage quote is attributed to the Hasidic rabbi Baal Shem Tov: "From every human being there rises a light that reaches straight to heaven, and when two souls that are designed to be together find each other, their streams of light flow together and a single, brighter light goes forth from their united being."

PERSIAN Rumi's thirteenth-century "Blessing the Marriage" poem: "This marriage be wine with halvah, honey dissolving in milk / This marriage be the leaves and fruit of a date tree / This marriage be women laughing together for days on end / This marriage, a sign for us to study / This marriage, beauty / This marriage, a moon in a light blue sky."

WELSH "Wishing you a house full of sunshine, hearts full of cheer, and love that grows deeper each day of the year."

From You to Your Guests

Guests love it when newlyweds express their affection for each other, and one or both of you should feel welcome to give a toast sharing your joy, thanking everyone for coming, and marveling at all the loving people in your lives. Here are some culturally specific ways to do that.

ARMENIAN "May your joys be as deep as the ocean and your misfortunes as light as the foam."

BIBLICAL "The Lord bless you and keep you! The Lord let his face shine upon you, and be gracious to you! The Lord look upon you kindly and give you peace!" (Numbers 6:24–26).

IRISH "Friends and relatives, so fond and dear, 'tis our greatest pleasure to have you here. When many years this day has passed, fondest memories will always last. So we drink a cup of Irish mead, and ask God's blessing in your hour of need." The traditional response to this toast is as follows: "On this special day, our wish to you, the goodness of the old, the best of the new. God bless you both who drink this mead, may it always fill your every need."

JEWISH A simple *l'chaim*, or "to life," works beautifully, whether as a blessing from you to your guests or vice versa.

SCOTTISH "Wherever you live in the world so wide, we wish you a nook on the sunny side, with much love and little care, a little purse with money to spare, your own little hearth when day is spent, in a little house with hearts content."

TAG, YOU'RE IT

Some couples ask that no one snaps photos during their wedding, but most want to see as many pictures as quickly as possible. If that's you, come up with a hashtag so that photos posted on social media are easy to find. Try a few versions that combine your names (#BeckysGetting Murrayed, if Becky Mickel is marrying Danny Murray), use the date (#LuckyThirteen, if you're making it official on the 13th), or make a pun involving the locale (#HappilyMauied, for a destination event in Hawaii). If you're not using a hashtag, a fun and/or auspicious tagline can be printed on programs, welcome bags, menus—any place type is welcome.

CHAPTER TEN

EAT, DRINK, LOVE

Delicious, Auspicious Eats

F ood nourishes luck. In addition to being tasty, the fare served at your wedding can also be spiced with significance, whether it's a beloved dish in your culture or a global symbol of abundance or sweetness. Keep in mind that you two now constitute a microculture unto itself; any food that brought you closer together definitely counts as lucky. If your first date was brunch, consider a morning wedding and a prosecco-and-pancakes reception. If you met in line at the ice cream truck, pass mini cones late night. Delicious food always makes us feel loved. Knowing it's meaningful is the cherry on top.

FORTUNATE FOODS

If you're a sweet-talking couple, you might be able to develop an entire menu out of nicknames you call each other. But if lamb chop followed by honey pie doesn't have your mouth watering, scan the following list. Some options are culturally specific; others are universal. Pick whichever ones whet your appetite.

APPLES In the Croatian countryside, wedding guests used to walk around the church's well three times, throwing in apples to invite fertility. A variation on this custom has the bride tossing apples over the roof of her house.

CANDY Sweets are a symbol of—you guessed it!—a sweet life. Jews throw candy at the groom (and, in Reform communities, the bride) at the *aufruf,* or "calling up," which takes place on the Shabbat before the wedding for Ashkenazi Jews or the one after for Sephardim.

CLAMS These are beloved at Japanese weddings because their shells are joined together—and they recall the clamshell given to represent longevity during the *yuino* engagement ceremony (see page 21).

CONCH A sign of virility and an aphrodisiac, conch are a mainstay at Caribbean weddings.

CORN Corn and cornmeal are fertility symbols central to many Native American wedding traditions. Couples may receive baskets of corn as gifts, and willow baskets of cornmeal are blessed during the ceremony, where they are set facing east, the most sacred direction.

EGGS Symbols of fecundity, eggs are given to couples as ritual gifts in many Islamic cultures and were once a traditional pre-wedding present in Jamaica, where they were meant to be used in the wedding cake.

FISH In China, fish is lucky because the word for fish (*yú*) sounds similar to the one for abundance (*yù*). But in Greece, where seafood is traditionally served at funeral meals, it's considered unlucky.

GRAPES Cross-culturally speaking, both fruits and seeds are fertility symbols. It's no surprise then that these seeded fruits were given to newlyweds in ancient Greece in the hopes that they'd be blessed with children.

HONEY Since refined sugar was once scarce, honey may be the original symbol of a sweet life. Guests at Moroccan weddings are offered honey before the ceremony, and Indonesian couples feed each other honey as part of their vow exchange.

LOBSTER This crustacean is popular in China because its shell, when cooked, turns red, the auspicious wedding color (see page 65).

NOODLES Long pasta is lucky for East Asians because the shape heralds a long life. For this reason, noodles are eaten both at weddings and at Chinese New Year banquets.

PINEAPPLE A whole pineapple has been a symbol of wealth and hospitality since explorers and missionaries brought them back to Europe and the United States from their tropical travels. Offering the delicacy to a guest was a sign of respect and welcome, which has led to pineapple-shaped door knockers and décor.

POMEGRANATES These are considered auspicious because of the sheer number of seeds they contain, signifying abundance.

RICE Whether it's being served at dinner or tossed at newlyweds post-ceremony, this grain is meant to invite fertility (see page 119).

ROE Planning a sushi station during cocktail hour? In Japan, fish eggs are a sign of many children to come.

WALNUTS Nuts, like seeds, are fertility totems. In the Mediterranean, walnuts are especially auspicious, as they break into four parts, representing the newlyweds and their families.

WHEAT In bread, crackers, and even as décor in centerpieces, this grain is a cross-cultural symbol of abundance.

WINE Not only is this beverage made of crushed fertility symbols, it's also a sign of joy and revelry, and has been since ancient festivals for Dionysus, the Greek god of wine. Plus, when shared by the couple from a common cup during the ceremony, it represents a joint future.

CEREMONIAL SNACKS

Many cultures don't wait until the reception to eat—some don't even hold out for the wedding itself. Among the Iroquois, pre-wedding prep involved the bride-to-be and her mother bringing maize cakes to the home of the groom. He returned the favor by handing them venison to show that he would be a good provider.

Ritual food or drink also plays a part in many wedding ceremonies. Jewish and Orthodox Christian couples sip wine from a common cup (see page 112), but in cultures where drinking alcohol is forbidden or uncommon, another beverage represents the sharing of the newlyweds' lives: in Bangladesh, it's *borhani,* a yogurt drink; in Java, it's sweet tea. Also in Java, the couple feed each other white and yellow rice spiced with turmeric, a sign of plenty, each eating three times. Navajo couples eat from the same basket of cornmeal mush to conclude the ceremony. Among the Yoruba community in Africa, the pair perform a ritual called "tasting the elements," sampling a wedge of lemon, a drop of vinegar, a pinch of cayenne, and a spoonful of honey to show they are prepared to experience the sour, bitter, spicy, and sweet sides of life together. In Nigeria and other parts of Africa, newlyweds exchange kola nuts after the vows, as symbols of fertility and of healing, because the nuts are often used in medicinal preparations. The exchange represents the couple's commitment to help heal each other's pain.

Arguably the most elaborate ritual food display in a ceremony is the Persian *sofreh aghd,* or "wedding spread," which includes seven herbs and seven pastries, plus bread, cheese, and greens (for life-giving nourishment); eggs, nuts, pomegranates, grapes, and apples (for fertility); and rosewater, rock candy, and honey (for sweetness). The goodies are distributed to guests after the ceremony.

LET'S GET THIS PARTY STARTED

Virtually every reception incorporates the ritual of sharing food, whether in a simple toast or an elaborate bread ceremony. At a Lithuanian wedding party, the parents of the newlyweds give them bread, wine, honey, and salt, so that they will always have nourishment, joy, and sweetness, and so that their marriage will endure, as if preserved by the salt. The same symbolic elements are found all over Eastern Europe: at a Polish reception, both sets of parents sprinkle bread with salt and offer it to the couple, followed by wine; in Russia, the bride's folks give her bread and salt as she leaves home; in Bulgaria, the groom's mom greets the newlyweds at the party with wine and a loaf of honey-drizzled *pitka* (see page 53). Many cultures bake special breads exclusively for weddings, such as the Polish, Russian, and Ukrainian *korovai,* which is covered in flowers, sheaves of wheat, lovebirds, and other lucky symbols.

The reception meal itself is a symbolic ritual, the first time the newlyweds join a community as a married couple. It's also a chance for the hosts, whether that's the newlyweds or their parents, to offer hospitality.

Specific dishes are synonymous with weddings. German receptions start with *hochzeitssuppe,* a chicken and meatball noodle soup reserved for important occasions because it takes so long to make—the name means "wedding soup." In Korea, the wedding reception is called the *kook soo sang,* or "noodle banquet," and the entrée served is *janchiguksu,* or "celebration noodles." In Japan, where red and white are wedding colors (see page 65), on-palette meals are popular—red rice and white sea bream, or red tuna and white rice. Sea bream is doubly lucky because its name, *tai,* sounds like the word for "fortunate." Peking duck is auspicious in China, because it's reddish and ducks mate for life—or until they become entrées. Even leftovers can be lucky: in China, guests are given red to-go containers to bring extras home.

HAVE A DRINK

Booze is also central to many a wedding party. In a ritual called *p'ye-baek*, a Korean bride will serve her new in-laws dates and chestnuts, which represent children, before they pour her a drink in return, usually *cheongju* rice wine, or a clear alcohol called *soju*, as a symbol of shared joy. The parents may then throw nuts and fruit for the bride to catch in her skirt. While this ritual traditionally took place in the days after the wedding, now it is often a spirited add-on to a reception. In England, the reception was referred to as a "bride's ale," because ale was the beverage usually served; this nickname is thought to be the genesis of the word *bridal*.

Today, the signature drink at a reception is whatever the couple choose or invent—it may be a cocktail they shared on their first date, or a twist on their favorite highball, spiced with a lucky herb.

And while your honeymoon is sure to include foods of all kinds, the word itself may come from the ancient Celts, who had newlyweds spend a month alone drinking fermented mead, also known as honey wine, which was thought to promote fertility.

TAKE THE CAKE

Given the cross-cultural identification of wheat with fertility and sugar or honey with wishes for a sweet life, it shouldn't be surprising that dessert, and especially wedding cake, is a huge part of the celebration. But there's no need to wait for the wedding. Chinese couples announce their engagement by having the groom's family send small cakes in red boxes stamped with the Double Happiness symbol (see page 87), or the sign for five sons and two daughters, which is considered the luckiest type of family. In Japan, the bride's family sends announcement cakes. Czech couples used to give *kolache,* round jam-filled pastries, as invitations—a good-luck sign because of their circle shape (see page 88).

In ancient Greece, it took three days to bake a wedding cake and, after it was shared by the guests, the leftovers were crumbled over the newlyweds' heads to bring them progeny and wealth. An ancient Roman groom would break a savory cake made of wheat (see page 136) over the bride's head to symbolize the end of her old life, before passing it out to attendees. In Scotland, this ritual was performed with oatcakes, again to invoke fertility and a break with the past—and to show the groom's dominance over the bride, which may be why the custom died. In medieval England, guests would bring sweet buns to the wedding and stack them in a pile the couple would stand on either side of and try to kiss over; if they reach each other over the stack, they were sure to have a prosperous life.

There are competing theories as to how the tiered cake came to be. One holds that a baker in seventeenth-century France frosted a tower of sweet buns, starting a trend. The other has an eighteenth-century London baker named William Rich taking inspiration from the spires of St. Bride's Church to create a towering confection to impress his bride. A multi-tiered marvel doesn't have to be your default. The following desserts have been considered auspicious for centuries.

BAUMKUCHEN A round confection with a hole in the middle, reminiscent of a ring, this German honey-and-almond delicacy is made by rolling layers of batter around a large skewer and baking them on the spit. (In an example of cross-cultural pollination, *baumkuchen* was introduced to Japan by a German baker, and is now a popular favor at Japanese weddings.)

BRUDLAUPSKLING A Norwegian delicacy dating back to when white flour was rare, expensive, and, therefore, a real treat, this cake is actually a stack of white bread layered with cream cheese and syrup—a dream come true for the couple who loves French toast.

CROQUEMBOUCHE French wedding cakes are really pyramids of cream puffs stacked and linked by caramelized sugar. The name means "crunching in the mouth," and while the confection is ceremoniously "cut" by the bride and groom, it's usually plated with each guest getting three or four individual cream puffs.

FRUITCAKE This dense, alcohol-soaked delight is the classic British wedding cake; Prince William and Kate Middleton had an eight-tiered version. Traditionally, the top tier, called the "christening layer," is saved for the baptism of the couple's first child—a custom that works a lot better with a dense fruit cake pickled in alcohol than the airy, egg-rich white cake that is popular in the United States. Fruitcake is also popular all over the Caribbean, especially in countries that were once under British rule.

KRANSEKAKE The Danish, Norwegian, and Icelandic wedding dessert known as "wreath cake" is a cone of almond-pastry rings iced with white glaze. The hollow center of the tower may be filled with a bottle of wine or aquavit or other treats, such as chocolate candies.

KUE LAPIS SURABAYA In Indonesia, ethnic Chinese couples cut this three-layer cake, whose shape represents the ladder to success, from the bottom, not the top, to represent their climbing to great heights together. After feeding each other, the newlyweds feed cake to their parents and grandparents as a show of filial love and respect.

LOVE CAKE A Sri Lankan delicacy served at weddings and sliced and given as favors, this is made with a plethora of fertility symbols (semolina, eggs, almond essence, cashews), sweet ingredients (sugar, honey), and spice (*doce de chila* pumpkin preserves, cloves, cinnamon, cardamom, vanilla, and rose water).

MILLEFOGLIE A traditional Italian wedding treat that invites abundance, *millefoglie* gets its name from the "thousand leaves" of phyllo-like pastry that are stacked to make it. There aren't really one thousand of them, but there is a lot of flaky goodness layered between mascarpone cream, fruit, or chocolate.

ŠAKOTIS For this Lithuanian dessert, dough is made of butter, egg whites, sugar, flour, and cream, then dripped over a rotating spit to cook. It ends up looking like a cake-colored evergreen, which makes it doubly lucky and gives it its name, meaning "branched tree" (see page 86). The branches may be covered in chocolate or sugar flowers.

JUST FOR HIM

A tradition that originated in Victorian England, the groom's cake, devoted to the man of the hour, is now more commonly seen in the Southern United States, where the custom became popular in the nineteenth century. While the most famous of all may be the armadillo-shaped, red-velvet monstrosity in the movie *Steel Magnolias,* a groom's cake is usually shaped or decorated to reflect his interests; you might have a basketball for an athlete or a dinosaur for a paleontologist. The groom's cake can be any flavor the gentleman prefers, but are often chocolate, to complement a white wedding cake. The groom gets his own cake in Bermuda, too, where it's traditionally a pound cake frosted in gold leaf to show his wealth, and topped with the cedar sapling the pair will plant in their yard (see page 103).

TOP IT OFF

A cake topper may seem like gilding the lily—how can a multi-tiered, frosted tower of sugary goodness need embellishment? But it's definitely classic. This tradition goes back to Queen Victoria, who crowned her cake with figurines of herself and Prince Albert. But bride and groom statuettes are not your only option. In Bermuda, cakes may hold a moongate, a mini replica of the coral arches prevalent throughout the island, meant to recall the full moon. The couple often passes through a life-size moon gate while holding hands on their way to the reception to show unity and invite happiness. You could top your cake with any lucky symbol (lovebirds, say), or one that feels auspicious to you (your married monogram).

MORE IS MORE

If you're loyal to another type of dessert, cake isn't the only auspicious choice. Here are some cultural favorites for serving as a final course or filling a dessert buffet.

BÁNH XU XÊ This Vietnamese dessert, called "conjugal cake," is a sticky ball of tapioca and mung beans wrapped in a banana leaf that mimics how the newlyweds will stick together. Yellow tapioca in the middle indicates the "golden heart" within each of them.

CSÖRÖGE "Angel's wings" in Hungarian, *csöröge* is fried dough that has been twisted in ribbons, and topped with confectioners' sugar.

DIPLES In Greece, these fried dough twists, whose name means doubles, are popular because each individual member of the couple is now doubled up.

FOY THONG In Thailand, the wedding dessert is *foy thong,* or "golden silk threads," made from egg yolks and sugar syrup pulled into long, noodle-like strips to represent long life. Foy thong may be served on its own or as a topping for a cake.

LIAN ZI Chinese wedding feasts end with this honey-and-lotus-seed treat meant to invite both sweetness and fertility.

WANDA A popular Italian wedding dessert, this confectioners' sugar-topped fried dough is shaped like bows to symbolize tying the knot.

CHAPTER ELEVEN

FAVORS
& FAREWELLS

*End Your Party—and Start Your Life—
on an Auspicious Note*

All ceremonies come with "musts" that you can't be married without—a vow exchange or legal contract, for example. But each culture has a few national customs that make the reception truly feel like a wedding, rather than any other party, and that also signal the celebration is coming to a conclusion. Those may be ritual dances that get all generations out on the floor, parting favors given to guests as a show of appreciation, or a dramatic getaway that offers everyone a chance to cheer, laugh, and say good-bye as the bride and groom ride off into the sunset together. A wedding takes so much planning, and is so much fun while it lasts. But the finale of the party shouldn't be seen as an ending. Instead, it's the beginning of a lucky new life together.

DANCE FEVER

Most weddings involve dancing, both the ritual kind and the party-on variety. At a Western reception, the significant numbers may be the newlyweds' first dance as a couple, the bride's turn with her father, and the groom's dance with his mother, symbols of the newlyweds leaving their parents' homes to join each other and build a new one together. In other cultures, the bride or groom performs a solo dance: a Samoan reception may kick off with the bride doing the traditional *siva*, and end with a group number called the *taualuga*, which is danced to celebrate the end of a major project, like the building of a house—or getting married. A Palestinian Arab groom may dance with a sword as a show of manhood and to demonstrate his ability to protect his bride, and she will do a candle dance, stepping onto the floor carrying a lit, decorated taper (see page 84), to be joined by her mother, mother-in-law, and other female guests in a candlelit procession.

In New Zealand, everyone may join in a *ngeri haka,* an expressive, stamping, shouting war dance that has become a way to show respect and deep emotion. It wouldn't be a Jewish wedding without the *hora,* a folk dance with Romanian origins that involves guests forming one or more circles, rushing toward each other to meet in the middle, retreating, and moving forward again. It's said that the coming together, apart, and together again reflects the rhythm of a long marriage.

In old Czechoslovakia, the bride's married female relatives did a raucous dance to amuse her, while in Finland, the bride, her mother, or godmother would dance with a plate balanced on her head. When it fell and broke, the number of pieces it shattered into foretold the number of children the couple would have. To this day, Jewish parents marrying off their last single child may take part in the *mezinke,* in which they sit in the middle of a circle while everyone dances around them and the

newlyweds crown them with floral wreaths, as the Yiddish tune "Die Mezinke Ausgegeben," or "The Youngest Is Given Away," plays.

The money dance is a ritual found in cultural groups ranging from Cajuns to Poles to Filipinos in which men line up to dance with the bride (and sometimes, women with the groom), and pay for the privilege, either pinning bills on the couple's clothing or handing them to the maid of honor to collect in a bag made for that purpose (called *la borsa* by Italians). In an interesting twist, at Czech weddings until recently, the maid of honor would dance holding a plate in her arms, as if it were a baby, as guests threw money, which was later given to the couple. This act is clearly a fertility ritual, but otherwise, a money dance is just a tangible symbol of the guests' good wishes for the couple.

To encourage cutting loose, adopt the Venezuelan, now pan-Latin, custom of the *hora loca,* or "crazy hour," in which the band cranks up the music and sends stilt-walkers, dancers, clowns, or armfuls of treats into the crowd toward the party's end.

DO THEM A FAVOR

So much attention is focused on the two of you, it can be a relief to think about other people. That's where favors come in. This small gesture allows you to thank guests for their support, and enables them to bring home a bit of the magic of the day. A favor can be anything from a little gift, like picture frames, to cards indicating that a donation has been made to a charitable organization on guests' behalf, to edible treats.

The tradition dates back to medieval times, when attendees at weddings were given boxes filled with sugar cubes or sweets called *bonbonnières* (which is still the word for "favors" in languages from French to Greek). Mexican wedding cookies are delicious balls of rich, buttery, sugary magic that are favors at—wait for it—Mexican weddings. A shortbread and nut treat that can be made with almonds, walnuts, or pecans, they're dusted with powdered sugar which gives them their Spanish name, *polvorónes,* or "dusty ones." In Brazil, the favor of choice is *bem casados* (whose name means "well-married" in Portuguese), mini sponge cakes sandwiching *dulce de leche,* jam, or egg curd. At Korean weddings, the standard takeaway is a gift box of three to five *dduk,* sweet bean–filled, sesame seed–covered rice cakes that can be tinted various colors and molded into shapes, such as flowers or hearts. They're so pretty that they're often displayed as a dessert buffet as well. The favors passed out at Japanese weddings are *kohaku manjyu,* steamed sweet buns filled with red bean paste. *Kohaku* means "red and white"—the traditional Japanese

wedding colors—and the treats are usually packaged in pairs, with one piece being red on the outside, and the other, white (see page 89).

Jordan almonds, also known as dragées, are the go-to in many cultures because they're both bitter and sweet, like life itself. A Dutch custom had guests gathering at the bride's house the day before the wedding to offer well wishes to the couple, eat *bruid suikas* ("bride sweets," aka Jordan almonds) and drink *bruidstranen,* mulled wine flecked with gold and silver leaf said to represent "bride's tears," the drink's name. Today, bruid suikas and bruidstranen are passed out at the reception, and packaged for guests to take home. (If you can't get your hands on bruidstranen, mini bottles of wine or champagne are another way to keep the celebration going, and happy tears flowing.) In Italy, the candy-covered nuts, called *confetti* in Italian, are wrapped in tulle bags for guests; each one holds five Jordan almonds to represent the five blessings everyone wishes for the newlyweds and the couple hope for their guests: health, fertility, longevity, happiness, and wealth. In some parts of the country, the bride and groom go from table to table distributing them and greeting loved ones. The Greek name for the culturally fluid Jordan almonds is *koufeta* and they're everywhere at weddings, from a tray on the altar at the ceremony to favors at the reception. Greeks make sure each decorative bundle holds dragées in a number that is prime (3, 5, 7, 11, or 13), so that it's indivisible, as the newlyweds should be. It's said that if single guests sleep with koufeta under their pillows, they'll dream of their future spouses. A similar, if messier, tradition takes place in England and its colonies where fruitcake is the customary favor taken home by guests, and mailed to those who could not attend, and is tucked under the pillows of unmarried romantics. Put your own spin on the custom by sending guests home with your favorite indulgence—for eating, not hiding under their pillows—whether it's late-night pizza, bagels for the next morning, or your mom's chocolate chip cookies.

Edible goodness isn't the only way to send guests away with smiles on their faces. At Puerto Rican weddings, attendees are given *capias*, decorative pins trailing ribbons printed with the couple's name and wedding date. This corsage-like keepsake identifies the wearer as someone who watched and supports the wedding; capias are also distributed at baptisms, first communions, *quinceañeras,* and other rites of passage. The bride may go around greeting her guests and pinning the capias on them, or the pins may be arranged on the dress of a doll wearing a miniature version of her gown so everyone can pick up their own. Another option is for the capias to be pinned to the ribbons of the bridal bouquet. In Thailand, guests receive floral garlands, and in India, it's ropes of jasmine, which they can tie around their wrists, ankles, or in their hair (see page 100).

If you prefer to give something practical as well as lucky, consider spices or salt (which add flavor and preserve food, the way love does life). Candles are also a symbol of your love that guests can use to add light and warmth to their homes (see page 84). Virtually anything can be made even more meaningful if it's personalized. Stamp tags with "thank you," "cheers," or a blessing or catchphrase in your native (or favorite) language.

AND AWAY YOU GO!

Some weddings end with a bang, with a raucous last dance, fireworks going off, or the couple leaving as guests wave sparklers (see page 84). Others wrap up with a cultural ceremony. German couples combine good luck with a good workout in a tradition called *baumstamm sägen,* or "sawing the log." The newlyweds use a two-handled saw to do just that, practicing working together.

If you're leaving in a getaway car—and there's a long history of doing so, as archaeologists have found ancient Greek pottery showing newlyweds racing off in flower-bedecked chariots—it might have something tied to the bumper. In the United States, that traditionally means tin cans clattering away. In the United Kingdom, it's shoes, which were once thrown at the couple as they tried to leave. It's believed that this practice is related to bride-kidnappings, when the abductee's family would lob things at the fleeing groom. The shoe-throwing evolved into tying them onto the bumper of the newlyweds' carriage or car for several reasons: First, the noise of the dragging shoes repels evil spirits. Second, they represent the couple walking into a new stage of life. And finally, it's one more chance for a fertility totem, if you add baby shoes. In Russia, guests tie a doll on the hood of the car to make sure the newlyweds have a child right away.

While everyone enjoys seeing the bride and groom off, several cultures drum up obstacles to prevent the newlyweds from making it to their house so that the celebration doesn't have to end. In parts of Japan, guests hold a rope to block the couple's door until they pay a toll. In Germany, chains of flowers and red ribbons are used to keep the pair at the reception unless they pay a ransom or promise guests another party.

Once you finally get to your house, chances are you'll think about one of you carrying the other over the threshold. It's a custom that dates back to the ancient Romans, who believed carrying the bride inside would protect her from any evil spirits hovering on the ground. Another traditional safeguard is to bring bread, wine, and salt into your home so you'll always have food, drink, and joy, and so that life will always have flavor. These useful pantry items are common housewarming gifts in Jewish, Russian, Eastern European, and Italian cultures, among others. What *not* to bring? An American wives' tale warns homeowners not to take an old broom into a new house; a new broom will sweep out any existing bad mojo.

In some cultures, it's not bad luck you have to worry about following you, but your friends. In China, the newlyweds' crew crams into the bridal suite to make noise, scaring away evil spirits until the couple kicks them out. In rural France, a similar ritual, called a *chiverie,* involves the pals banging pots and pans and ringing bells outside the door until they get invited in for more food and drink. The custom, rarely practiced today, morphed into a shivaree among the Cajuns in Louisiana.

When you make it safely inside, you may want to cut into a tier of your wedding cake—Haitians do, so the fruitcake will bring fertility into their house. Or consider following a tradition from Bermuda, and planting a tree that will grow along with you. In Switzerland, the couple's friends plant a tree in their yard, so that the newlyweds will have wood to make a cradle.

AND THEY LIVED LUCKILY EVER AFTER

Just because your wedding is over doesn't mean you should stop looking for creative ways to celebrate love and attract luck. Many married couples keep a souvenir of a meaningful wedding ritual in their home, whether it's their framed ketubah for a Jewish couple or, for Orthodox Christians, a carved round wooden frame called a *stefanothiki* holding their wedding crowns. There are even holidays devoted to making sure your spouse enjoys good fortune. In northern India during the festival of Karwa Chauth—which usually falls in late October or early November— women fast from sunrise to moonrise, praying that their husbands will enjoy a long life, until they spot the moon's reflection in water or through a sieve, make an offering to the moon, then turn to see their spouses standing behind them. In recent years, men have started returning the favor, so that the couple fast for each other's luck. That may inspire you to spend a day together, say a prayer, or to feed each other moon pies— when it comes to rituals, the details matter less than the sentiment behind them. Whatever your background, you'll find the most tried-and-true good-luck ritual of all is telling each other how lucky you are to have found each other, and doing so as often as possible.

Acknowledgments

Folklore has so much to teach us, but its greatest lesson is that none of us lives in a vacuum. Supportive communities make life's joys richer and sorrows bearable. And the support of countless friends, relatives, and colleagues made this book possible.

First, thanks to my aunts for reading my future in coffee grounds; Eleni Nikolaides, for wrapping all the bonbonnières for my wedding and filling my life with love; and to my parents, sister Marina, cousin Efrosini, and my cousins on Corfu and new relatives in Nicaragua for throwing me not one but two weddings (in the same day!). Thanks to my husband, Emilio, our children, Amalia and Nico, and their cousin, Stone, for three great baptisms; and my friends for the everyday rituals and celebrations that give life meaning.

Friends from a multitude of cultures provided both the inspiration for, and the fact checking of, many rituals in this book. Notable among them are Neela Pania and Vimla Pania, who discussed Hindu theology at length, and Katherine Fausset and Kay Fausset, who gave me the tip about burying bourbon that inspired me to inter an airplane nip of brandy at the Corfu Sailing Club.

Many thanks to my former colleagues at *Martha Stewart Weddings,* for feeding my obsession with nuptials, teaching me so much, and encouraging me in this process—and for publishing my story that was the original inspiration for this book. Specifically, thanks to Michael McCormack for your support, design advice, and generally being in the room where it happened; Jen Cress for your intel and enthusiasm; Amy Conway for the assignment; Darcy Miller, who shows us all how to celebrate everything; and Elizabeth Graves for being a constant source of friendship and inspiration.

It takes a village to raise a book, and my editor Amanda Englander and her assistant, Gabrielle van Tassel, have been wonderful godparents. Thanks, too, to Terry Deal, Jenny Jimenez, and Mia Johnson at Clarkson Potter. Emily Isabella's artwork brought the beauty of these rituals to life in a way words alone never could. My agent, Stéphanie Abou, is the first person I told about this idea. She responded with all the support I have now come to expect from her. Stéphanie, finding you was *bashert*. Last, but definitely not least, thanks to Jenny Zamora, for nurturing my children while I wrote this.

And to everyone whose wedding I danced at, or who danced at mine: thanks for sharing the joy. You make me feel very lucky indeed.

Works Referenced

Allen, Kimberly Burton. *Wedding Wonder: Tales & Traditions, Customs & Curiosities*. Glendale Heights, IL: Great Quotations Publishing Company, 1967.

Arnold, Elliott. *Blood Brother*. Lincoln: University of Nebraska Press, 1979 (first published 1947).

BenShea, Noah. *A World of Ways to Say "I Do": Wedding Vows, Readings, Poems, and Customs from Different Traditions and Cultures*. New York: McGraw Hill, 2005.

Cerullo, Christina. *The Bride's Pocket Guide to Wedding Customs and Superstitions*. Brookfield, CT: Sinematrix, 2011.

Dundes, Alan. *The Study of Folklore*. Englewood Cliffs, NJ: Prentice-Hall, Inc., 1965.

Editors of *Martha Stewart Weddings*. *Martha Stewart Weddings: Ideas and Inspiration*. New York: Clarkson Potter/Publishers, 2015.

Elleven, Russell K. *Reverent Rituals: A Brief Wedding Guide*. New York: iUniverse, 2003.

Fitzgerald, F. Scott. *F. Scott Fitzgerald: A Life in Letters: A New Collection Edited and Annotated by Matthew J. Bruccoli*. New York: Scribner, 1995.

Goodridge, Hillary. *Hillary Goodridge & others vs. Department of Public Health & another,* Supreme Judicial Court of Massachusetts, November 18, 2003, available at caselaw.findlaw.com/ma-supreme-judicial-court/1447056.html.

Gourse, Leslie. *Native American Courtship and Marriage Traditions*. New York: Hippocrene Books, 1995.

Homer and Alexander Pope. *The Iliad*. Seattle: Amazon Classics, 2017.

Ingpen, Robert R., and Philip Wilkerson. *A Celebration of Customs and Rituals of the World*. New York: Facts on File, 1996.

Jones, K. C. *Fortune-Telling Book for Brides*. San Francisco: Chronicle Books, 2009.

Jones, Leslie. *Happy Is the Bride the Sun Shines On: Wedding Beliefs, Customs, and Traditions*. New York: McGraw-Hill Education, 1995.

The New American Bible, Revised Edition. New York: HarperCollins Publishers, 2012.

Oring, Elliott, ed. *Folk Groups and Folklore Genres: A Reader*. Logan: Utah State University Press, 1989.

Roney, Carley. *The Knot Guide to Wedding Vows and Traditions: Readings, Rituals, Music, Dances, and Toasts*. New York: Clarkson Potter/Publishers, 2013.

Rouvelas, Marilyn. *A Guide to Greek Traditions and Customs in America*. Bethesda, MD: Attica Press, 1993.

Schultz, Christine. "Why Are Wedding Dresses White?" *The Old Farmer's Almanac*. Dublin, NH: Yankee Publishing, 2018.

Spangenberg, Lisl M. *Timeless Traditions: A Couple's Guide to Wedding Customs Around the World*. New York: Universe, 2001.

Thomas, Daniel Lindsey, and Lucy Blayney. *Kentucky Superstitions*. Princeton: Princeton University Press, 1920.

Tresiddor, Jack. *1,001 Symbols: An Illustrated Guide to Imagery and Its Meaning*. San Francisco: Chronicle Books, 2004.

Various Authors. *Every Woman's Encyclopaedia*. London, UK: London S.N., 1910–1912.

Warne, Frederick. *Flower Fairies. The Meaning of Flowers: Folklore, Fairylore, Superstitions, Remedies*. London, UK: Penguin Books, 1996.

INDEX

About the Author

The daughter of a Greek father and a Minnesotan mother, Eleni N. Gage graduated from Harvard University with a degree in folkore and mythology before pursuing a career in magazine journalism and earning an MFA in creative writing from Columbia University. As a writer and editor, she worked at *Allure, Elle, InStyle*, and *People* magazines, and was the executive editor of *Martha Stewart Weddings*.

The author of the travel memoir *North of Ithaka* and the novels *Other Waters* and *The Ladies of Managua*, Eleni is now a contributor to *Martha Stewart Living* and a freelance writer whose work has appeared in publications ranging from *The Wall Street Journal* to *Travel + Leisure*.

Fulfilling the predictions of an Indian astrologer who told her that she'd marry a "soft-hearted businessman who wasn't born in the United States," Eleni is the wife of a Nicaraguan coffee trader and the mother of two Greekaraguan children. They live in New York City, and bake a magic cake every year on New Year's Day to attract good luck.